MODEL DRAWING
GEOMETRICAL AND PERSPECTIVE
WITH ARCHITECTURAL EXAMPLES

a 2

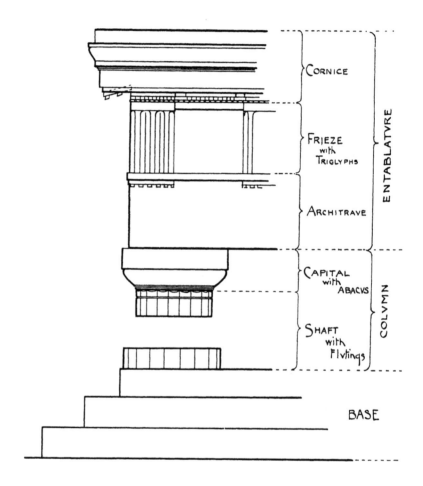

CORNICE

FRIEZE
with
TRIGLYPHS

ARCHITRAVE

CAPITAL
with
ABACVS

SHAFT
with
Flvtings

ENTABLATVRE

COLVMN

BASE

DORIC

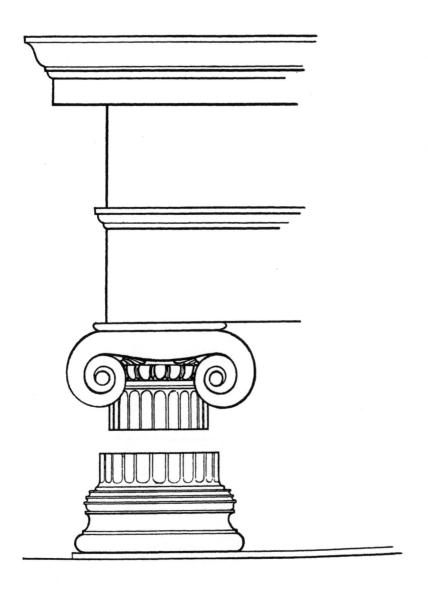

IONIC

MODEL DRAWING

GEOMETRICAL AND PERSPECTIVE

WITH ARCHITECTURAL EXAMPLES

BY

C. OCTAVIUS WRIGHT

Art Master's Certificate (Board of Education)

AND

W. ARTHUR RUDD, M.A.

Late Scholar of St John's College, Cambridge

(Assistant Masters at Abingdon School)

ILLUSTRATED BY OVER 300 DIAGRAMS

Cambridge:

at the University Press

1916

CAMBRIDGE
UNIVERSITY PRESS

University Printing House, Cambridge CB2 8BS, United Kingdom

Cambridge University Press is part of the University of Cambridge.

It furthers the University's mission by disseminating knowledge in the pursuit of education, learning and research at the highest international levels of excellence.

www.cambridge.org
Information on this title: www.cambridge.org/9781107505582

© Cambridge University Press 1916

First published 1916
First paperback edition 2015

A catalogue record for this publication is available from the British Library

ISBN 978-1-107-50558-2 Paperback

PREFACE

LONG experience in the teaching of Model Drawing has convinced the authors that the use of the ordinary apparatus of the art—the cube, the sphere and other formal geometrical models—fails in most cases to arouse the interest of the student or to inspire him with the imagination which is essential to the development of artistic talent.

An experiment was made in the employment of architectural forms with the customary models, and the success which has attended this experiment has encouraged the authors to a systematic treatment of the subject, and to its presentation through this volume to a larger public.

Although in the present treatment of the subject there will be found an undercurrent of suggestion of the historical develop ment of architecture, the work is not intended to be an architectural text-book. If it is found to be of value in presenting in an interesting form the theory of correct drawing, and in acting as an incentive to original work, the object of its production will have been attained.

Apart from its use of architectural forms the book contains several new features. No measuring points are employed. Useful perspective tests are introduced which with a little practice can be applied with facility, and should be of great benefit to the student in his more advanced work. The authors believe that the perspective treatment of the circle is quite new, and they have found that pupils can use the method with ease and advantage. Comparisons of representations on changing picture planes are given, and their relative advantages are discussed. Frequent opportunities are afforded for sketching from memory. Free use is indicated of tracing-paper in observation work, and of clay in modelling.

C. O. W.

W. A. R.

June 1916.

CONTENTS

ILLUSTRATIONS

PART I. (Geometrical)

Chapter I. Rectangles

PART II. (Perspective)

Chapter V. Rectangles

'To distinguish between correctness of drawing and that part which respects the imagination, we may say the one approaches to the mechanical, and the other to the poetical. To encourage a solid and vigorous course of study, it may not be amiss to suggest, that perhaps a confidence in the mechanic produces a boldness in the poetic.'

Sir JOSHUA REYNOLDS
(13th Discourse).

A SURVEY

The earliest known examples of art are the figures of animals drawn by cave-men. These drawings gave birth to the art of writing. Architecture, however, seems to have arisen from the worship of mighty stones, and it was through this reverence that the Egyptians built the great pyramids as everlasting resting-places for the dead.

The art of building seems first to have grown to strength in the valleys of the Nile and Tigris, and the art of the valley of the Tigris may have been prior to that of Egypt. More is known, however, of the origin of the buildings of Egypt than of those of Western Asia, and it is therefore with Egypt that the story of architecture begins.

A few years ago it was thought that no Egyptian work existed of a date prior to that of the *Great Pyramid* (p. 80) of the fourth dynasty, but recently much work of the first three dynasties has been found. The earliest tombs took the form of almost solid masses in rough brick whose walls leaned inwards; and the finest tomb of this type which has been explored is at Meydum, where the first pyramid proper is found.

There is a connection between these rough brick tombs or *mastabas* (p. 194) and the later pyramids; the primitive grave developed into the mastaba. This was transformed into the step-pyramid, which developed naturally into the final or perfect form of the true pyramid. The Great Pyramid is practically a great mastaba.

As early as the beginning of the dynasties, the vault, the dome, and the arch appear in Egypt. An arch in its simplest form is the upper part of a horizontal hollow in a mass of clay or gravel. The vault was thought of as a continuous convex shell, although it was produced by the addition of cakes of mud of equal size. It was this uniform vault which later under the Romans became the basis of the magnificent concrete construction of that people. The wedge arch might quite naturally have had a separate origin. Children have often been observed to make experiments in bridging empty spaces, and similar experiments might well have accounted for the origin of the true arch of masonry which is not found in Egypt except as a later development after the brick arch had existed for some 2000 years.

Arches frequently appear on the Assyrian slabs. The art of the valley of the Tigris, as early as the eighth and ninth centuries B.C., displays many similarities to Greek art; and in later days strong and constant Greek influence may be seen in the art of Western Asia. Though in Egypt, Babylon, and Crete there were three different centres of early civilization representing three different continents, architecture is usually considered to a large extent an Egyptian art.

The first appearance of European art is shown to have been in the islands of the Aegean with its centre at Crete, and discoveries show clearly that there was at that time communication between this civilization and that of Egypt. Remarkable finds have been made recently in Crete pointing to a very highly developed culture; and round tombs with beehive domes found here closely resemble the *chambers* (p. 80) in some Egyptian pyramids. The chambered mounds of Brittany probably belong to the period of these pyramids; and possibly Stonehenge, which is not savage but built of wrought stone, has something of the same style in it.

No direct connection has been found between early Aegean art and Greek art, but it seems that it was for Greece to undertake the task of collecting and perfecting the gifts of Egypt. The most remarkable feature of Greek art is the rapidity of its rise to its zenith, and of its subsequent decline.

Greek architecture has two modes, the *Doric* (Frontispiece) and the *Ionic* (Frontispiece), names which correspond to those of 'native' and 'colonial,' or 'old' and 'new.' The typical *plan of a Doric temple* (p. 47) with a cella having a portico is derived from the architecture of the Aegean age. The curious Doric frieze with its *triglyphs* (p. 93) follows an old type of slab construction, and the cornice is an eaves-course of projecting rafter ends copied in stone. The older Parthenon at Athens was a fine example of seventh century Doric architecture. The Ionic style was more slender and graceful than the vigorous and masculine Doric. Its chief characteristic was a capital which was cut not from a square block but from a block which was longer one way than the other, the ends being curved into a spiral. The Ionic cornice with its *dentils* (p. 48) is simply a rendering in stone of the over-hanging part of a flat roof.

The most famous example of Greek art at its highest development is the Parthenon, which was completed about 435 B.C. The Ionic order was probably adopted about the middle of the sixth century B.C. From a highly enriched form of the Ionic was evolved the luxurious *Corinthian order* (p. 171), an interesting example of which is the monument of Lysicrates at Athens.

To the Greeks we owe the most perfect type of tomb, also of theatres, and of stoae or covered colonnades; and to descend to detail it is to their invention or improvement that we owe the modern mosaic floor, panelled doors, the *spiral stairway* (p. 174), and the turned legs of furniture. Nor, of course, are the gifts of Greece to the world confined to the list just given: for through Rome and Roman civilization Greece handed on some of its influence to the whole of Europe.

The debt of Rome to Greece, in this as in all the other arts, needs no proof; she received her gifts especially through the medium of Sicily where magnificent schools of architecture existed from an early period. When Rome had acquired all she desired of Greek art she soon outstripped all competitors, and in the first and second centuries A.D. she became the mistress of the world and the centre of its culture. Engineering, particularly military engineering, is the prominent feature in her architecture, and as such it is peculiarly rich in hints to modern builders, who may gather from her work methods of vaulting in concrete, and of building with pots and pipes, and even 'tricks of the trade' such as the use of crushed brick in mortar. The most typical Roman work was in concrete, and all the greatest buildings of Rome were faced with plaster.

1—2

Ecclesiastical buildings form the most interesting branch of Roman architecture. The early church consisted of a fore-court, a nave with pillars, and an apse. This plan is called 'basilican'; a Roman basilica, or justice-hall, had very nearly this form, and the word 'basilica' seems to have had a general meaning much as our word 'hall.' However, the basilica was afterwards enclosed like a temple and adapted to various uses. A temple of rectangular plan found in Samothrace, an island of the Aegean, has been called by some writers the real prototype of the Christian basilica.

After the Peace of the Church in the fourth century Christian edifices were built all over the Empire. The Church of the Holy Nativity at Bethlehem is the most perfect early Christian church still existing. The remains of a small basilican church of this time have been recently unearthed at Silchester, near Reading.

Early Christian art leads to Byzantine art. Byzantium, or Constantinople, was from 330 A.D. the capital of the Eastern Empire, and in the sixth century was the centre of the arts; its greatest work is the church of Santa Sophia built by Justinian about 537 A.D. In recent times a large number of carved capitals has been discovered in Egypt, and these are so much like those found in Santa Sophia that it is only reasonable to assume some connection between them. It is quite probable that the school of carving which developed the Byzantine capitals was transferred to Constantinople from Egypt by Justinian. Several new architectural ideas were due to Byzantine builders. They gathered into groups windows with arched heads, they set moulded courses on walls, and they introduced the use of *corbel tables* (p. 66). The early Christian and Byzantine schools made the column carry the arch, and made the capital a bearing block of supreme beauty.

The change between antiquity and mediaevalism is seen at the age of Romanesque art,—the change from Roman art to Gothic art,—the turning-point in which seems to have coincided with the establishment of the power of Charlemagne in the ninth century.

In the fifth century the Gothic art spread from east of the Rhine over the whole Western Empire. In England, at the end of the sixth century, civilization came with the Church, and it is in this age, in which Santa Sophia was built, that we place the

famous legends of King Arthur and his knights. In Gaul the
arts were probably practised much as in Italy, and about 600 A.D.
a school was founded in England. A school of building which
rapidly developed in the eleventh century was that in Normandy.
The Tower of London is a fine example of its work. Features
of Norman architecture worthy of note are the banding and
chequering (p. 56) of two different coloured stones, and the introduction of the type of plan in which chapels surround the apse.

Christian churches were once more built in this country after
the beginning of the seventh century. St Wilfrid built one at
Hexham, King Alfred one at Athelney, and an abbey church at
Abingdon was founded in 675. Up to about 900 Saxon architecture would seem to have been mainly derived from early
Christian and Byzantine examples. It seems probable that a
special Eastern influence may have been introduced by some early
monk, as patterns exhibiting the *braided decoration* (p. 103) known
all over Europe in the eighth and ninth centuries in book ornamentation, and in stone carving, appear in Saxon England at an early
date. The *half-quatrefoil* (p. 107) and *trefoil* (p. 102) arches also,
which are probably Eastern in origin, appear in Saxon works—
the trefoil, for example, is found on the side door of Ely Cathedral.

With the rebuilding by Edward the Confessor in 1050–66 of
Westminster Abbey the Norman form of Romanesque appears in
England, and the English-Norman art took a leading part in the
progress of architecture to the Gothic. More churches were built
in England between 1050 and 1150 than in any other country.
The early part of the twelfth century was a time of great architectural activity, and several of the schools at this time seem to
have attempted to attain to the leadership. With the settlement
however of the centre of mediaeval thought and art at Paris, the
race was decided in her favour, and with this period begins the
most interesting epoch in the history of architecture, namely that
of the Gothic style.

It is not easy to explain in words what perfect Gothic art is.
It is frank, clear, energetic, and healthy. Some may perhaps
understand it through the metaphor of one writer who regards
a cathedral as it were so 'highly strung' that if struck it would
give out a musical note. In Gothic art the idea of a building

with walls simply pierced for light, and supporting the burden
of the roof, gives place to the feeling of a structure continuous
throughout and energetic in every part. The wall rose up into
tense shafts and piers from which soared forth the ribs of the
vault (p. 239). The windows became *mullioned* (p. 68) and *traceried*
(p. 109), and the body a cage of stone. The earliest building
properly to be called 'Gothic' is the abbey church of St Denis,
near Paris, begun in 1140, followed by the cathedrals of Paris and
Rheims.

It is from this parent French art that English Gothic was
derived. Early English Gothic ends in 1350, the time of the
terrible visitation of the Black Death after whose gloom the arts
never recovered their former sweetness. At this date Later
Gothic begins and two centuries before and after give the beginning and the end of English Gothic, in 1150 and 1550.

A somewhat detailed arrangement of the periods of English
Romanesque and Gothic art together with a chronological table
is given at the end of this survey.

The ruling feature of English Gothic at its highest is a spirit
of sweetness which contrasts with the grandeur of the towering
spires of France: its special contributions to the traditions of
mediaeval Gothic art were the *octagonal chapter-house* (p. 59), the
working out of several fine varieties of *open timber roofs* (p. 81),
and the early elaboration of curvilinear tracery.

When the mediaeval culture matured, Italy was the most
learned country in Europe. Its artists and scholars were in daily
contact with the monuments of the past, and they naturally turned
back to the glory of Rome that had been. The Renaissance in
Italy therefore was a natural impulse, and the fashion, which had
grown up in Europe, of imitating the most forward country com-
pelled other countries to follow the lead of Italy. However, the
Roman revival or renaissance has, as a whole, proved quite
barren, and has left no offshoot.

Splendid works were wrought even in its dull maturity by
Michael Angelo, Wren, and Inigo Jones; but in general the
Renaissance style seems a style of boredom. The chief works
that had to be built in this country were not temples with
columns, but palaces with enclosing walls. In these structures

the principal features were naturally windows, floors, and staircases, which were precisely the details for which there was least authority.

The Renaissance indeed had in a sense a mission to give a full explanation of the first principles of all arts, and Roman architecture was largely an art based on first principles. It is therefore in modern engineering,—almost entirely an art of first principles, —that we have to look for the most splendid architectural product of the Renaissance.

TABLE A.

Style	Date	
Saxon	1000	Romanesque
Early Norman	1050	
Mature Norman	1100	
First Gothic	1150	Early
Lancet	1200	
Geometrical	1250	
Curvilinear	1300	
Black Death	1350	Gothic
Late Decorated	1350	Late
Mature Perpendicular	1400	
Rectilinear	1450	
Tudor	1500	
Elizabethan	1550	
Renaissance	1600–1650	

8

A SURVEY

TABLE B.

B.C.			
3000	Egyptian	First Egyptian Dynasty
		Arch and dome on slabs
2000	... ...	Third Egyptian Dynasty
		Great Pyramid
1500	... ...	Cretan art at highest
1000	... ...	True arch of masonry
900	Greek	Greek art emerges
550	... ...	First Ionic building
435	... ...	Parthenon built
400	... ...	Greek art blossoms
A.D.		
1	Roman	Greek art decays
200	... ...	Roman art at highest
300	Early Christian ...	Churches built in Europe
327	... ...	Church of Holy Nativity built
537	Byzantine	Santa Sophia built
600	... ...	School in England
675	... ...	Churches built at Abingdon, Hexham and Athelney
800	Romanesque	Charlemagne reigns
974	... ...	Winchester Cathedral begun
1000	... ...	School in Normandy
1050	... ...	Westminster Abbey begun
1150	Gothic in England ...	Plantagenets, 1154
1250	... ...	Magna Carta, 1215
1350	... ...	Black Death
1450	... ...	Fall of Constantinople
1530	Renaissance in England	Tudors
1675	... ...	St Paul's Cathedral begun

PART I

CHAPTER I

RECTANGLES

Take a piece of paper as in fig. 1 and fold it over as in fig. 2, making a crease AB. Then fold the paper again so that the point A exactly covers the point B and mark the creases OC, OD as in fig. 3.

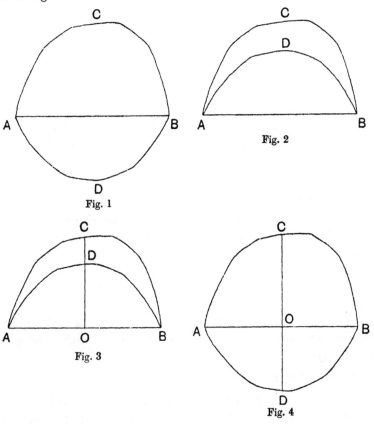

Fig. 1

Fig. 2

Fig. 3

Fig. 4

If the paper be now unfolded, two straight creases will be seen crossing one another at O as in fig. 4.

What can you say about the angles AOC, COB, BOD, DOA? Refer to fig. 3.

If two straight lines AB and CD intersect at a point O, so that the four angles AOC, COB, BOD, DOA are all equal, each of those angles is called *a right angle*.

How can you draw such an angle?

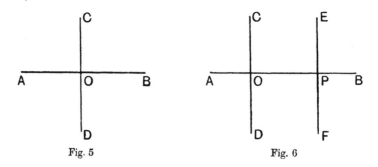

Fig. 5　　　　　　　　　Fig. 6

Draw such a pair of straight lines and at any other point P in AB draw another straight line EPF at right angles to AB. Then the straight lines CD and EF, being drawn in the same direction, are said to be *parallel* to one another.

How do you draw two parallel straight lines?

Examples of parallel straight lines may easily be found, especially in woodwork, of which the plank with its parallel edges forms the basis. In stonework also parallel straight lines occur resembling those of woodwork, of which they must be regarded as imitations, since it is natural to assume that accurate workmanship in wood preceded that in stone.

Now draw two straight lines AB and DC parallel to one another, and another pair, viz. AD and BC, at right angles to AB or DC.

Are AD and BC parallel to one another?

The figure $ABCD$ is called a *rectangle* and AC and BD are said to be its *diagonals*. Let AC and BD intersect at the point O.

Then O is the *centre* of the rectangle, and the dotted lines through O parallel to AB and AD bisect the sides of the rectangle.

What do you know concerning the relation between the lengths of AD and BC? of AB and DC? and of AC and BD?

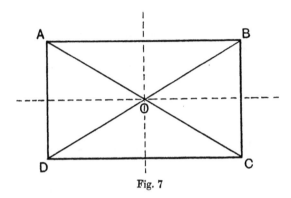

Fig. 7

The rectangle, or oblong, as it is commonly called, is suggested by the forms of many artificial objects. Roofs, floors with their planks and tiles, walls with their bricks and stones, doors with their panels, and domestic windows with their divisions, afford examples.

In practice we test the right angles which their sides contain by set squares, T-squares or try-squares, and thus secure a complete fitting of parts in such structural work.

The figure is a plane surface and we shall see later that the geometrical solids we are about to consider contain plane and curved surfaces.

The planeness of a surface may be tested by a straight-edge. Among the ruins of early Egyptian buildings spots of red paint have been found on the faces of the stones. It is probable that these surfaces were tested by bringing them into contact with a reddened plane. The Egyptian builders aimed at great accuracy in workmanship. The casing stones of some of their pyramids show such correct fitting that the film of mortar left between them is on an average not thicker than one's thumb-nail.

In all that we do to-day, we still have no reason to despise accuracy.

Draw any rectangle $ABCD$ and its diagonal BD.

What do you know about the areas of the figures ABD and BCD?

Now draw any straight line POQ parallel to AB intersecting the diagonal in O and through O draw a straight line ROS parallel to AD as in the figure.

What do you know concerning the areas ROB, QOB? and concerning the areas POD, SOD?

Putting these facts together, can you state any relation between the rectangles $PARO$ and $SOQC$?

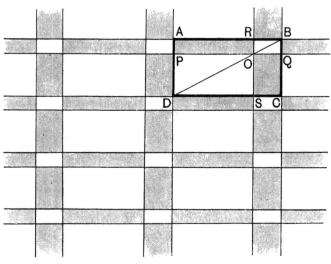

Fig. 8

The number of units of area in a rectangle is expressed by the product of the number of units of length and the number of units of breadth. Thus the rectangles whose measurements are $4'' \times 3''$ and $6'' \times 2''$ have an area of 12 square inches.

Copy the accompanying figure, making the complete rectangle $2'' \times 1''$ and the broader shaded strip $\frac{1}{4}''$ wide.

   (i)   What is the width of the narrower shaded strip?

   (ii)   Is the rectangle symmetrical about a diagonal?

Symmetry shows in flat treatment a doubling of a form about a straight line as axis, and in the case of solids about a plane. It is a means of producing ornament. In nature absolute symmetry rarely occurs, but there is generally a balance of parts.

In the rectangle divided as in the figure there is a balance of parts without symmetry and this method of division can be made use of in the decorative treatment of rectangular areas.

The floor of a church, its entrance front, vaulted roof, arcades, and traceried windows may be symmetrical. Its east to west aspect may show balance without symmetry, but symmetry may be evident in its north to south aspect.

Suggestions for Practical Work

1. Cut out several rectangles, each $1'' \times \frac{3}{8}''$, from brown and white paper. Arrange as in figures 27–30 and paste on cardboard.

2. Cut out several strips, $6'' \times \frac{3}{8}''$, from brown and white paper and arrange to represent basketwork.

3. Cut out a number of rectangles, each $1'' \times 2''$, from stiff paper to represent tiles. Make holes in them to show the holes through which they would be nailed to the framework of the roof.

Arrange these tiles on your drawing-board as in a roof, beginning at the bottom and working upwards.

DIRECTION

We will now explain how certain directions in space may be fixed and other directions compared with them.

Suppose a piece of cotton, with a weight attached to it, to be suspended from a fixed point and allowed to hang freely. The direction of the cotton is said to be *vertical*. If a straight line AB be drawn through a point O in the cotton at right angles to this direction, AB is *horizontal*.

Let us imagine AB as a wire fixed with wax to the cotton and let us suppose the latter to twist round about P, the point of suspension, whilst AB remains at right angles to the cotton. The wire AB will lie in a *horizontal plane* and the straight line OP, which is at right angles to every straight line passing through the point O and lying in the plane, is said to be at right angles to the plane.

How would you test whether a given straight line is vertical? whether a given plane is horizontal?

Any plane which contains the straight line OP is called a *vertical plane*. We can clearly draw any number of these planes, so that whilst we can draw through a point O only one horizontal plane we can draw through the same point an infinite number of vertical planes. All these planes are *at right angles* to this horizontal plane and to all other horizontal planes.

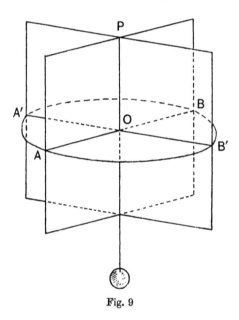

Fig. 9

How many vertical lines can you draw through a given point? how many horizontal lines?

How many vertical planes can you draw containing a given vertical straight line? how many horizontal planes containing a given horizontal straight line?

The planes to be found in buildings are generally either vertical or horizontal. The surfaces of walls and floors afford examples.

Practical Work

1. Out of a piece of stiff paper cut two equal rectangles A and B each 6″ long and 6″ broad. Join the middle points of opposite sides by straight lines. In both A and B cut halfway along one of these lines and one-quarter of the way from both ends along the other and fit A and B into one another as in fig. 10.

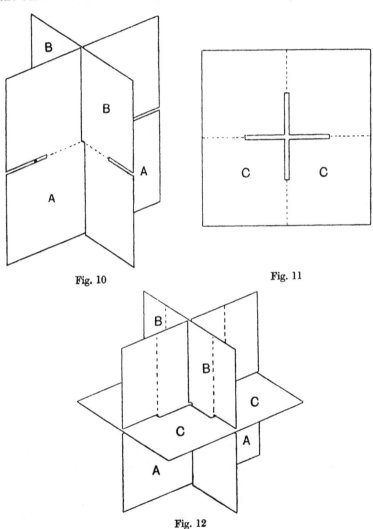

Fig. 10   Fig. 11

Fig. 12

Now cut out a third rectangle C, the same size as A and B, and draw the central lines as before. Cut along these lines from the centre leaving the outside halves uncut as in fig. 11. Bend back the upper flaps of A and B along the dotted lines, and slip C centrally over them when the upper parts of A and B may be again straightened out as in fig. 12. You now have represented three planes meeting at a point and such that each pair is at right angles.

If C be horizontal, what can you say about the planes A and B?

If C be vertical, can you say anything about the planes A and B?

2. Cut out a paper rectangle $ABCD$ 4″ long and 2″ broad and draw a diagonal AC. At A draw a straight line AE making an angle of 30° with the diagonal. Attach a weighted cotton to A and hold the rectangle so that, A being uppermost, the following lines are vertical by turns: (i) the side AB, (ii) the diagonal AC, (iii) the straight line AE, (iv) the side AD.

Is the plane of the rectangle vertical in each case?

3. Hang up two weights by means of two strings.

Are the strings parallel?

Are all vertical lines parallel?

Are the strings in the same plane?

PROJECTION

Suppose we are given a plane XYZ and a point A outside the plane and that we draw a straight line AA' at right angles to the plane meeting it in the point a.

The point a is called the *orthogonal projection* on the plane XYZ of the point A.

If you were to place your eye at any point in aA produced, at what point in the plane would the point A appear?

Consider now a straight line AB outside the plane and suppose straight lines AA' and BB' are drawn at right angles to the plane and meeting it in the points a and b. The straight line ab is called the *orthogonal projection* on the plane of the straight line AB, and if a perpendicular Pp be drawn to the plane from any point P in AB it will be found that the point p lies in the straight line ab.

The straight lines *Aa, Bb, Pp* are called the *projectors* of the points *A, B, P*.

If your eye were again placed at a point in *aA* produced the point *B* would not appear at the point *b* in the plane.

At what point in the plane would the point *B* appear if your eye were placed at *E*? at *F*?

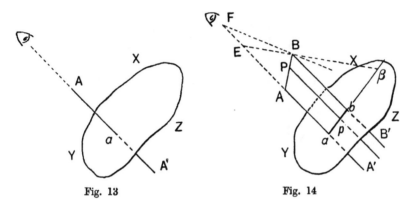

Fig. 13   Fig. 14

Suppose β to be the point in the plane at which *B* appears and that you move your eye further away from the plane along the straight line *aA*.

How does the point β move?

Could the point β coincide with the point *b* as *E* moves further away from the plane?

PLAN AND ELEVATION

If *ab* be the orthogonal projection of *AB* on a horizontal or ground plane, *ab* is the *plan* of *AB*; and if *a'b'* be the projection of *AB* on a vertical plane, *a'b'* is an *elevation* of *AB*.

How many different elevations of *AB* can be drawn?

How many different plans?

Let these two planes meet in the straight line *XY* as in fig. 15. Then *XY* may be called the *ground line*.

What are the heights of *a'* and *b'* above the ground line?

What are the distances of *a* and *b* from the ground line?

The plan and elevation are drawn on the same piece of paper. This is done by supposing one plane to rotate about the line XY until the two planes lie in one and the same plane, which is taken

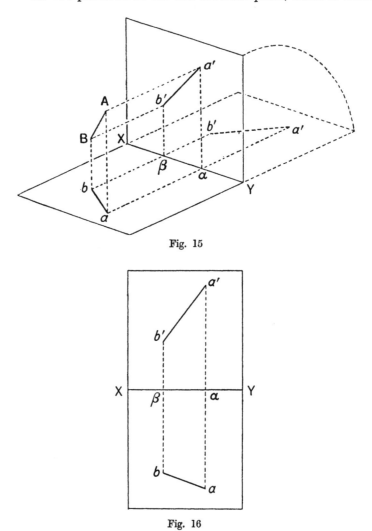

Fig. 15

Fig. 16

to be the plane of the paper. This is shown in fig. 15 and the drawing is made as in fig. 16. Here $b\beta b'$ and $a a a'$ are straight lines drawn perpendicular to XY, β and a being points in XY.

aa' and $\beta b'$ are the heights of A and B above the ground plane; aa and βb are their distances from the vertical plane.

In fig. 15 $ABba$ is a vertical plane and the angle which this vertical plane containing AB makes with the vertical plane of projection is the angle which ab makes with XY.

In future we shall refer to the horizontal and vertical planes of projection as the H.P. and the V.P. respectively.

When is the plan of a straight line AB represented by a point?
When is its elevation a point?
Can both the plan and elevation of AB be points?

Ex. A straight line AB, 1·5″ long, makes an angle of 60° with the H.P. and is in a vertical plane which makes an angle of 45° with the V.P. Draw its plan and elevation.

Draw a straight line XY (fig. 18), the intersection of the H.P. and the V.P., and draw a straight line OB making $Y\hat{O}B$ equal to 45°. Make $O\hat{B}A'$ equal to 60° and mark off BA' equal to 1·5″. Draw $A'a$ at right angles to OB.

Then aB is the plan of AB.

Draw aa and $B\beta$ at right angles to XY and produce aa to a' making aa' equal to $A'a$. Join $a'\beta$. Then $a'\beta$ is the elevation of AB.

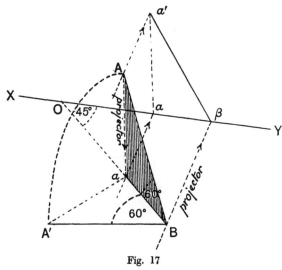

Fig. 17

2—2

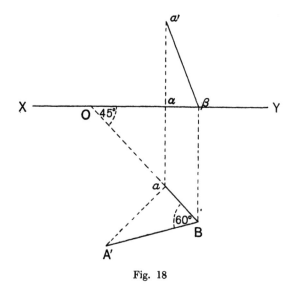

Fig. 18

Having seen how to find the plan and elevation of a straight line we can now project a figure which is bounded by straight lines.

Take a cardboard box without the lid and cut away one of the sides and both the ends, leaving only the small triangular pieces

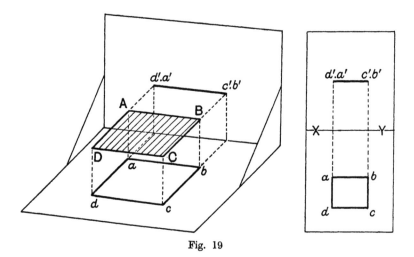

Fig. 19

shown in the figures, which will act as supports for the remaining side.

Consider this side and the bottom of the box as your planes of projection. Cut a rectangle *ABCD* out of one of the ends and hold it in the following positions:

(i)   In a plane parallel to the bottom of the box (the H.P.) and with its longer edges parallel to the ground line, as in fig. 19.

(ii)   In a plane parallel to the side of the box (the V.P.) and with its longer edges parallel to the ground line, as in fig. 20.

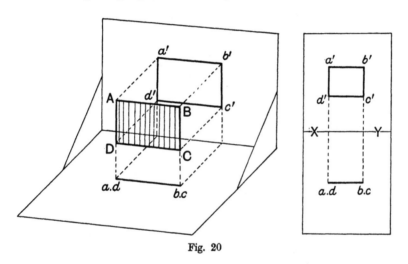

Fig. 20

Its plan and elevation are as shown and the figures explain themselves if you have grasped the idea of the projection of a straight line.

What would the plan and elevation be if the rectangle were held with its longer edges vertical and its shorter edges at right angles to the V.P.?

Carefully notice the notation adopted for those points in the plan and elevation which are the projections of more than one considered point of the rectangle.

Now hold the rectangle in the following additional positions:

(iii)   In a plane inclined to the H.P. and with its shorter edges at right angles to the V.P., as in fig. 21.

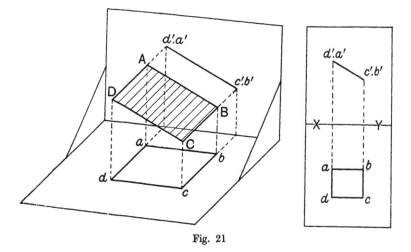

Fig. 21

(iv) In a plane inclined to the v.p. and with its shorter edges at right angles to the h.p., as in fig. 22.

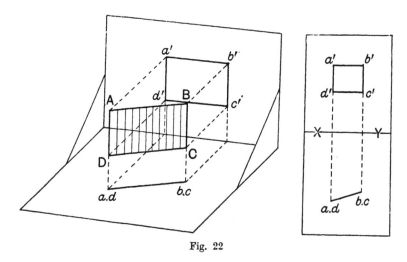

Fig. 22

Lastly, hold the rectangle with its longer edges horizontal and with its plane inclined to the h.p. and to the v.p.

What is its plan?
What is its elevation?

Ex. Let the angles of inclination to the H.P. and to the V.P. be each 45°. Draw the plan and elevation of the rectangle.

When is the plan of a plane figure a straight line?

When is the elevation a straight line?

Can both the plan and elevation be straight lines?

The plans of large isolated buildings are not as a rule easily discernible, but their simple elevations are. The plan controls the general effect of the whole from most points of view. Since this is the case, there should be a pleasing combination of effects from both plan and elevation.

Each may show an excellent balance of areas, but when a perspective view is deduced from these projections the result may be unfortunate. The plan need not be intricate, as simplicity often gives a noble and aesthetic effect. The plan of a Greek temple was simple and its elevation showed no great complexity in form. The temple was rectangular in plan, as were also the basilica and, later on, the parts of many of our cathedrals.

Simple Shadows

A source of light sends out in all directions rays of light which travel in straight lines through space. When these rays strike the surface of a body they render it bright but are usually stopped by the body so that none of them pass through it. Thus on the side of the body opposite to the source of light is a region through which these rays are not travelling. A surface interposed here will appear darker than if the rays of light are allowed to strike it, and the body is said *to cast a shadow* on the surface.

Pin a sheet of paper to your drawing-board and place it in a horizontal position. Hold a knitting-needle so that the shadow of the needle on the paper as cast by the sun is

(i)　　a point,

(ii)　　equal in length to the needle.

If you tilt your board, can you again arrange the needle so that the shadows are as in (i) and (ii)?

Now place the needle and board so that the shadow is of infinite length.

How do the sun's rays strike the board in this position?

Hold the needle in various positions so that its shadow falls on the paper.

What is the form of the shadow?

We infer that the shadow of a straight line on a plane surface is either a straight line or a point.

In future in speaking of shadows we refer to those cast by the sun's rays. The rays which strike any two points P and Q travel in straight lines and have their point of intersection in the sun at such a great distance from P and Q compared with the length of PQ that we may and do consider them parallel.

The shadow of an object on a plane is therefore a projection of the object by a set of parallel projectors which, in general, are not at right angles to the plane.

Practical Work

1. Push a knitting-needle through a stout card at right angles to it and hold the card in sunlight so that the knitting-needle casts no shadow on the card.

At what angle do the sun's rays meet the card?

Fix a pin to the knitting-needle at any angle by means of some wax and, holding the card as before, mark the position of the pin's shadow on the card.

Why is this shadow the orthogonal projection of the pin on the card?

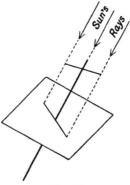

Fig. 23

2. Tie two strings of unequal length to the ends of a stick and fasten weights to the free ends of the strings. Hold the stick so that the weights just touch the ground.

What is the projection of the stick on the ground?

SHADOWS OF RECTANGLES

In the following figures we are considering rectangles in sunlight with their planes either at right angles to or parallel to the planes on which the shadows fall.

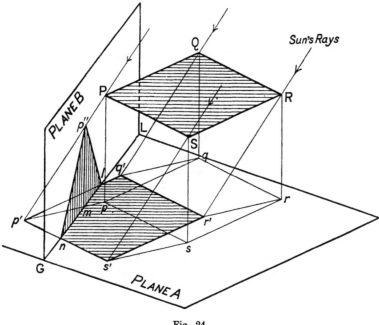

Fig. 24

The planes A and B shown in fig. 24 are at right angles to one another and intersect in the straight line GL.

$PQRS$ is a rectangle whose plane is parallel to the plane A and consequently at right angles to the plane B.

$pqrs$ is the orthogonal projection of the rectangle on the plane A and $p'q'r's'$ is its shadow on the same plane if the plane B be removed.

The straight lines Pp', Qq', Rr' and Ss' are parallel, and since the points P, Q, R and S lie in a plane which is parallel to the plane A their distances from that plane, viz. Pp, Qq, Rr and Ss, are equal.

Hence the obliques Pp', Qq', Rr' and Ss' are equal and it follows that $p'q'$ is equal and parallel to PQ, $q'r'$ is equal and parallel to QR, etc.

The shadow $p'q'r's'$ is therefore a rectangle whose sides are equal and parallel to the corresponding sides of $PQRS$.

Now suppose the plane B to be introduced and that GL intersects the edges $p'q'$ and $p's'$ of the shadow $p'q'r's'$ in the points l and n, and pp' in the point m.

Ppp' is a plane at right angles to the plane A and therefore meets the plane B in a straight line $p''m$ which is at right angles to GL, p'' being the point in which Pp' meets the plane B.

$p''l$ and $p''n$ are therefore the shadows on the plane B of those portions of PQ and PS which throw shadows $p'l$ and $p'n$ on the plane A.

In this position the shadow on the plane B is $p''ln$ and on the plane A is $lns'r'q'$.

Carefully notice that the traces on the planes A and B, i.e. the lines of intersection with these planes, of the planes passing through the sides of the rectangle $PQRS$ mark the limits of the shadow as cast on the two planes.

In fig. 25 $PQRS$ is a rectangle the plane of which is at right angles to the plane A. pq or sr is the orthogonal projection of the rectangle on the plane A and $p'q'r's'$ is its shadow on that plane if the plane B be removed.

The straight lines Pp', Qq', Rr' and Ss' are parallel, and since PQ and SR are parallel to the plane A it follows that $Pp = Qq$ and $Rr = Ss$.

Hence $Pp' = Qq'$ and $Rr' = Ss'$ and it follows that $p'q'$ is equal and parallel to PQ and that $r's'$ is equal and parallel to RS.

The shadow $p'q'r's'$ is therefore a parallelogram whose sides $p'q'$ and $r's'$ are equal and parallel to the corresponding sides of $PQRS$.

Now suppose the plane B to be introduced at right angles to the plane A and that their line of intersection GL meets the edges $s'p'$, $q'r'$, $s'r'$ of the shadow in the points l, m and n.

Ppp' and Qqq' are planes at right angles to the plane A and therefore meet the plane B in the straight lines $p''l$ and $q''m$, which are at right angles to GL, p'' and q'' being the points in which Pp' and Qq' meet the plane B.

If Rr' meets the plane B in the point r'', $p''q''$ and $q''r''$ are the shadows of PQ and QR on the plane B. $p''l$ and $r''n$ are the

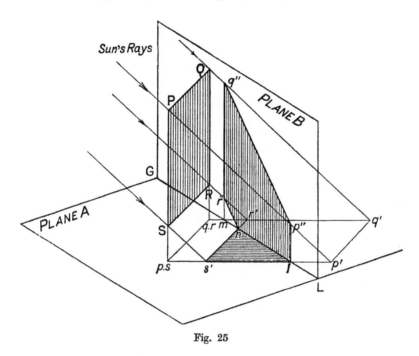

Fig. 25

shadows of those portions of PS and SR which throw shadows $p'l$ and $r'n$ on the plane A.

Here the shadow on the plane B is $lp''q''r''n$ and on the plane A is $ls'n$.

As in the previous argument we can show that $q''r''$ is equal and parallel to QR. This leads to an important fact in dealing with shadows, and it may be stated thus:

The shadow on a plane of a straight line which is parallel to the plane is equal and parallel to the straight line.

Practical Work

1. Fix on the point of a pen a small rectangular piece of squared paper. Place it in sunlight in a plane parallel to the plane of a piece of similarly squared paper on your drawing-board and mark the corners of the shadow.

Move the rectangle into planes parallel to the plane of the board so that one edge of the shadow remains fixed in position.

What do you notice about the other edges of the shadow and in what directions are the corners of the rectangle moving?

Rotate the rectangle about one edge so that the shadow remains rectangular.

In what positions are the areas of the shadows greatest and least?

Let the sun's rays fall perpendicularly on the board. Hold the rectangle so that its shadow is a straight line and is as long as possible.

How long is this line?

2. In a rectangular piece of stiff paper cut two rectangular openings to represent a doorway and a window. Fix it with plasticine at right angles to a piece of squared paper on your drawing-board and place your board in a horizontal position in sunlight. Arrange it so that the shadows of the edges of the openings are sides of rectangles.

Draw on the squared paper an angle which shows the inclination of the sun's rays.

Knowing this inclination determine the height of the window, which is supposed to be inaccessible.

Keeping your board horizontal rotate it and mark the shadows of the edges of the openings in two other positions.

What are your observations?

3. Bend in halves a sheet of squared paper and, fixing it with plasticine, arrange its two planes to represent the ground and a wall.

Cut a long rectangle of stiff paper and mark it to represent a ladder. Perforate it with a compass-point at the ends of each rung and then lean it against the wall.

Place all in sunlight, and on the ground and wall mark the bright spots and join them in pairs to represent the shadows of the rungs.

Do this in two positions and state the result of your observations.

Arrange the ladder so that the shadows of the side of the ladder on the ground and wall are of equal length.

What is the inclination of the ladder to the ground?

Rotate the ground plane.

Do the shadows of the side of the ladder remain of equal length?

Ex. A Greek cross (fig. 41) with arms 3″ long and ½″ wide stands on the ground in a vertical plane with one arm vertical. Show, in plan only, the shadow on the ground when the vertical plane containing the sun's rays is inclined at 45° to the plane of the cross, and the elevation of the sun is 60°.

RECTANGULAR FORMS

In working the following examples the T- and set-squares must be freely used, and accuracy and neatness in draughtsmanship are to be aimed at.

Example I. The Ground Plan of an English Church

Draw the plan of a cathedral (fig. 26), inserting the names of the chief subdivisions of the building. Let the length of the nave be 6″ and draw the rest of the plan to scale. Give a suggestive south-side elevation.

The plan of English churches is very frequently in the form of a Latin cross (fig. 42), in which the cross arms are the transepts. Of the other arms, the longer shows the position of the nave, and the shorter that of the chancel. In the figure there are given in addition the positions of the tower, aisles, choir, Lady-chapel, cloisters and garth of Salisbury Cathedral.

Our earliest churches date from the close of the seventh
century, when the abbey churches of Hexham and Abingdon
were built. Winchester Cathedral and the abbey church of
Ramsey were tenth century work, and were probably cruciform
in plan.

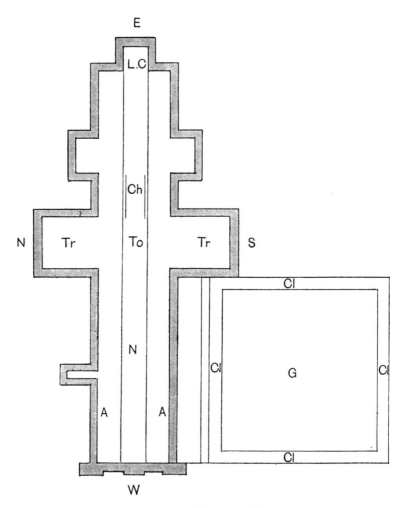

Fig. 26.　Plan of Salisbury Cathedral

N, Nave; A, Aisle; Tr, Transept; To, Tower; Ch, Choir; L.C, Lady-Chapel;
Cl, Cloisters; G, Garth

Example II.   Herring-Bone Work

(A)

Fig. 27.   Herring-Bone

Show the method of arranging herring-bone work.

Let each rectangle measure $\frac{1}{4}'' \times \frac{3}{4}''$ and draw sufficient to show the scheme of repetition.

Also draw, in plan only, the bricks lettered P, Q, R, S, T, V and W and give an elevation of them standing on the H.P. with the ground line parallel to the long sides of the brick P.   Let the bricks be half as high as they are long.

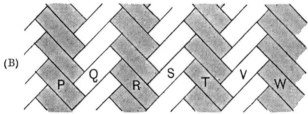

(B)

Fig. 28.   Herring-Bone

Herring-bone work consists of bricks arranged obliquely. Very irregular work of this kind has been found in Roman and occasionally in Norman walls, and in the latter instances the

(A)

Fig. 29.   Tiles

backbone is usually present. In more skilful work we find examples without the backbone, as between the beams in the half-timbered fronts of mediaeval domestic buildings.

Other arrangements of bricks are shown in figs. 29 and 30.

(B)

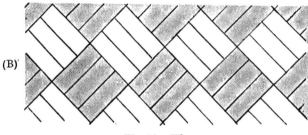

Fig. 30.   Tiles

Example III.   Rustication

Illustrate rustication (or rusticated masonry) showing at least four whole and four half stones.

Let each face measure $1'' \times \frac{1}{2}''$.

Suggest an elevation showing the channelling.

This is a kind of ornamental masonry, chiefly Classic and Renaissance, in which the corresponding faces of adjacent stones are separated by a broad channel which marks the joints between the stones. It is a peculiar feature of some of the fine palaces in Florence.

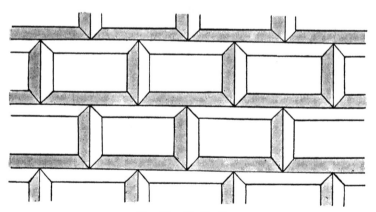

Fig. 31.   Rustication

Just as in Gothic work architects aimed at making everything ornamental, however mean its use, so in Renaissance work they aimed at concealment and uniformity.

Example IV.   Steps

Draw sections of steps as shown, making the angles of pitch 10°, 45° and 60°.

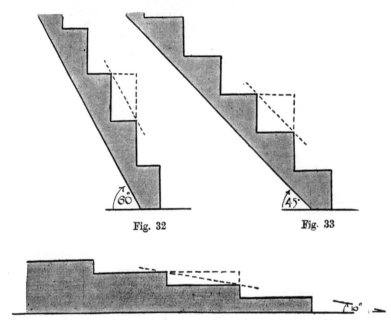

Fig. 32   Fig. 33

Fig. 34

Example V.   The Dentil Band

Draw a portion of a dentil band, showing about ten dentils and making each $\frac{1}{4}''$ wide.

This ornament, which resembles teeth, is freely used in the Ionic and Corinthian orders.

The origin of the band is doubtful, and it has been suggested that it is an imitation in stone of timber structure, but it is more probable that its prototype is found in rock-hewn tombs, as at Gizeh. Here the projecting eaves are cut into a series of half-rounds, probably to resemble small palm trunks. A fragment of one is to be seen in the British Museum.

Fig. 35. Dentil Band

Example VI. Long and Short Work

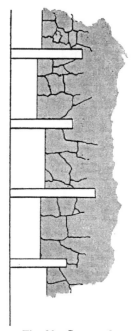

Reproduce the figure, making the long stones $1''$ and the short stones $\frac{1}{6}''$ high, and wash in the drawing as suggested.

In Saxon times the angles of buildings were sometimes strengthened by roughly squared masses of stone placed on each other so that the visible faces are alternately long and short. The main wall is of rubble masonry.

Fig. 36. Long and Short Work

Example VII. The Chain Band

Copy the figures, making the rectangles in figs. 37 and 39 $1'' \times 2''$ outside measurement, and the bands $\frac{1}{8}''$ wide, and the rectangles in fig. 38 half these dimensions.

This is composed of links which are either represented all in front view as in figs. 38 and 39 or alternately in profile as in fig. 37. The chain pattern occurs in many styles, affording a vigorous effect.

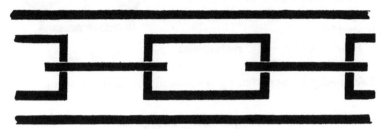

Fig. 37.   Chain Band

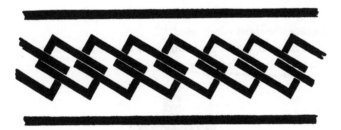

Fig. 38.   Chain Band

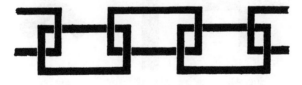

Fig. 39.   Chain Band

3—2

Example VIII. Interlacement

Copy the design, making the rectangles 1″ × 2″, outside measurement, and the bands ⅛″ wide.

The interlacement band includes all those bands which are formed of a number of lines inter- laced or plaited together. In the Celtic, Saxon and Norman styles it is the most conspicuous ornament.

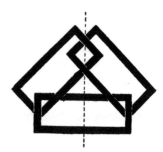

The Moorish style favours a peculiar interlacement, in which it is characteristic that the bands are always straight, and make angles of 90° or 135°.

Interlacement of rectangular links is shown in fig. 40. The axis

Fig. 40.   Linking

of symmetry is suggested by the dotted line in the drawing.

Example IX. The Cross

Draw the Greek, St Andrew's and Latin crosses, making the equal arms of the two former and the short arm of the latter each 2″ × ½″.

In design the cross symbolizes Christianity. The Greek and Latin crosses are most often used.

In a variety of forms it is found on vessels, garments, carpets and banners dedicated to religious uses.

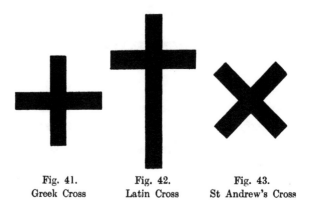

Fig. 41.   Fig. 42.   Fig. 43.
Greek Cross   Latin Cross   St Andrew's Cross

RECTANGULAR PRISMS

If a solid has every face a rectangle it is called a *rectangular prism*. Such a solid can have only six faces and at each corner there are three faces at right angles to one another as in fig. 12. [Consequently each pair of opposite faces constitutes a pair of parallel planes.] Many common objects are fashioned in this form, e.g. a brick, a plank, etc.

Name some other familiar objects which are rectangular prisms.

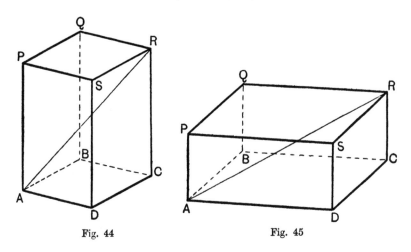

Fig. 44   Fig. 45

The prism has four diagonals, such as AR, which join opposite corners.

What can you say concerning these diagonals?

Let $ABCDPQRS$ (fig. 46) be a rectangular prism with one pair of faces horizontal. We may project the faces of the prism on the H.P. and on vertical planes. We thus obtain the plans and elevations of the faces, and the complete figures thus obtained are called the plan and elevations of the prism.

In the figure the faces $ABCD$ and $PQRS$ are horizontal, and we see how to obtain the plan L and two simple elevations M and N on two planes parallel respectively to the other faces of the prism.

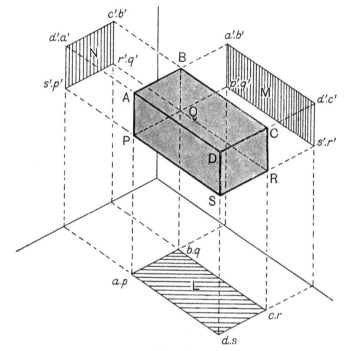

Fig. 46

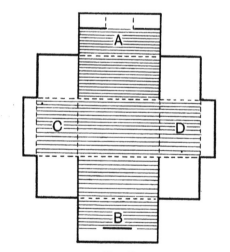

Fig. 47

Notice the notation at the corners of the plan and elevations and compare with figs. 19–22.

Cut a piece of stiff paper the same shape as shown in fig. 47. Cut along all the thick lines and bend the paper at right angles along the dotted lines. The shaded portions form the faces of a rectangular prism and the unshaded rectangles round C and D are the flaps to be tucked in. Bend back the flaps of A and slip this end through the opening B from above. The flaps of A will then open and hold the edges of the paper securely.

If your model is placed on a horizontal table and viewed (i) from the side, (ii) directly from above, how many faces are visible in each case?

What is the greatest number of faces that you can see at one and the same time?

Place your model on an H.P. and take the elevations on two V.P.s at right angles to one another (i) when the V.P.s are parallel to, and (ii) when the V.P.s make angles of 30° with, the vertical faces of the prism. The plan and elevations of (i) are shown in fig. 48 and of (ii) in fig. 49.

Ex. Twist your model on the H.P. until the angle 30° in fig. 49 becomes 45° and again draw the plan and two elevations.

It will be useful to consider here a simple section of a rectangular prism. In fig. 50 the prism is cut by a plane which bisects two adjacent faces and is parallel to their edge of intersection.

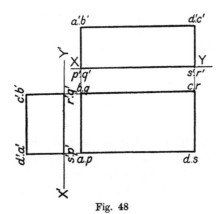

Fig. 48

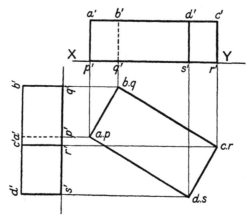

Fig. 49

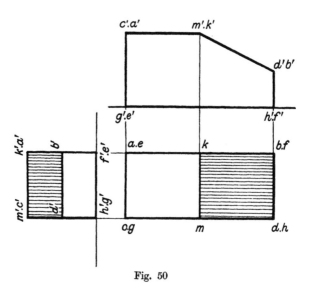

Fig. 50

When an edge of the prism is cut away by a plane parallel to that edge, the edge (or *arris*) is said to be *chamfered* (fig. 50).

In stonework and woodwork the edges are often treated in this manner, and the chamfered face generally makes equal angles with the two sides.

This is sometimes done for the purpose of avoiding the damage which might occur if the edges of the blocks were left sharp. The walling stones of a sixth century temple at Ephesus show chamfering, probably for this purpose.

SHADOWS OF RECTANGULAR PRISMS

In figs. 51 and 52 we have drawings of a rectangular prism *PQRSpqrs* with one face *pqrs* in contact with the plane *A*. The direction of the sun's rays is represented by the straight lines *Pp'*, *Qq'* and *Rr'*, *p'*, *q'* and *r'* being points in the plane.

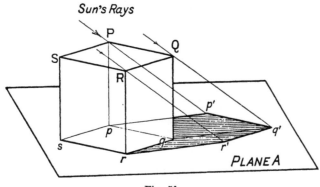

Fig. 51

Ppp', *Qqq'* and *Rrr'* are equal right-angled triangles in parallel planes, i.e. *pp'*, *qq'* and *rr'* are equal and parallel. Hence the figures *pqq'p'*, *qrr'q'* are parallelograms.

The shadow cast by the prism is the figure *pqrr'q'p'* and is the same as that cast by the two adjacent faces *PQqp* and *QRrq*, both of which are at right angles to the plane *A*.

Make similar drawings of a rectangular prism and its shadow upon a plane *A*. In fig. 51 introduce a plane *B* at right angles to the plane *A* and let the line of intersection of the two planes cut the edges *p'q'* and *q'r'* of the shadow. Construct *q''*, the point in which *Qq'* meets the plane *B*, and complete the shadow as cast on the two planes.

In fig. 52, which shows a block projecting from a wall, introduce a plane *B* at right angles to the plane *A* and let the line of intersection of the two planes cut the edges pp' and $q'r'$ of the shadow. Construct p'' and q'', the points in which Pp' and Qq' meet the plane B and complete the shadow as cast on the two planes.

Refer to figs. 24 and 25.

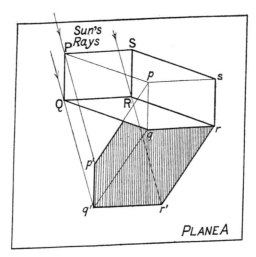

Fig. 52

Practical Work

Cut out to scale ($\frac{1}{2}$ cm. = 1 in.) in plasticine a brick $9'' \times 4\frac{1}{2}'' \times 2\frac{1}{2}''$. Stand it on one of its largest faces on a piece of squared paper on your drawing-board and place the whole in sunlight, arranging the board so that the entire shadow cast on the paper is a square whose side is equal to the longest side of the brick.

What is the inclination of the sun's rays to the board?

MODELLING

The following six examples are to be modelled in clay or any other suitable medium. Plans, elevations and perspective views are shown.

In each case one measurement is given, and to determine the remaining measurements a scale must be drawn.

Example I.   A Solid Letter H

In the adjoining plan *ab* represents 3″.   Draw a simple scale to determine the remaining measurements.

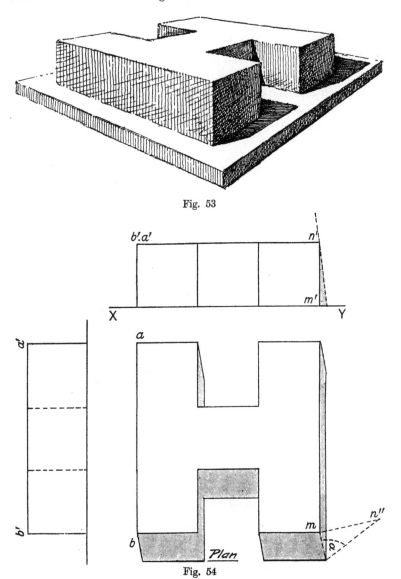

Fig. 53

Fig. 54

When you have constructed your model, place it in sunlight. Arrange it so that (i) the short side faces cast no shadows, (ii) the long side faces cast no shadows, (iii) there are no shadows, (iv) both pairs of side faces cast shadows.

Now with a modelling tool mark on the slab the shadow edges as found in position (iv). Take the model to your place.

Reproduce on paper the given plan of your model as it lies on its slab and draw in to scale the shadow edges. Wash in the shadow and after lettering the figure write down your conclusions. (The construction for finding the elevation a of the sun is shown in figs. 54 and 56.)

Example II. Post and Lintel

In the adjoining plan ab represents 4″.

The treatment of the shadows may be studied as in Example I.

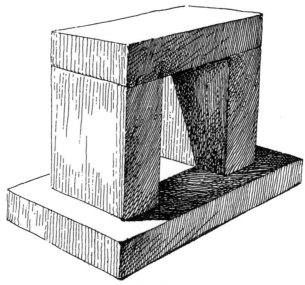

Fig. 55

A lintel is a piece of timber or stone spanning an opening, be it a door, or a window, or a space between columns.

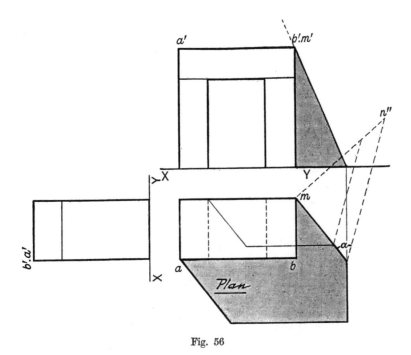

Fig. 56

Example III.　A Flight of Steps

In the adjoining plan *ab* represents 2″.

Fig. 57

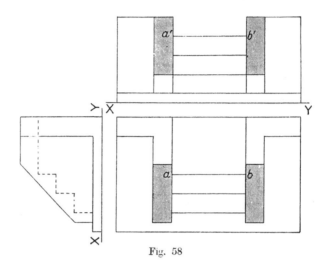

Fig. 58

Example IV. Brickwork

Arrange fifteen bricks in the manner shown, making each brick $9'' \times 4\frac{1}{2}'' \times 2\frac{1}{2}''$ ($\frac{1}{4}$ scale).

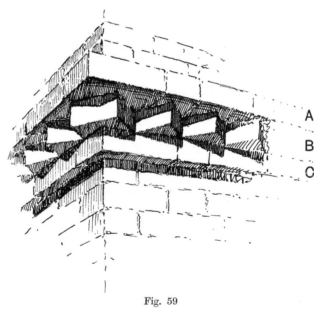

Fig. 59

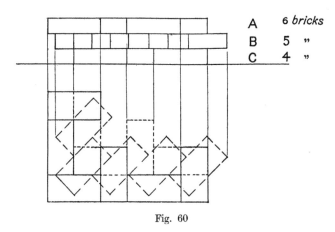

A	6 *bricks*
B	5 "
C	4 "

Fig. 60

Example V.　The Plan of a Greek Temple

In the adjoining plan *ab* represents 4″.

The Egyptians probably imagined that the earth was for them a rectangular slab and that the sky was a ceiling supported by four great pillars. In this image they constructed their temple to the extent that they decorated the slab with vegetation and the ceiling with celestial bodies.

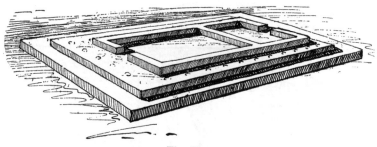

Fig. 61

The Greek temple stood open to the sun and air; it invited the admiration of the passer-by; its most telling features and best sculpture were on the exterior. A sacred cell was provided for the reception of the image of the divinity and usually another cell was added which served as a sacristy. The external rows of columns seem to have originated in a form of veranda added round the cells to guard their walls.

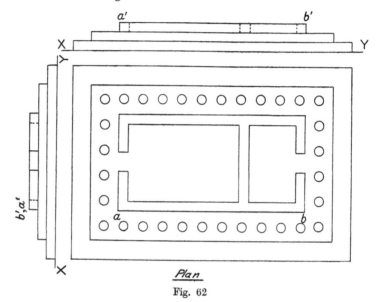

Plan
Fig. 62

Example VI.   The Dentil Band*

In the adjoining plan *ab* represents 5″.

Fig. 63
* See p. 33.

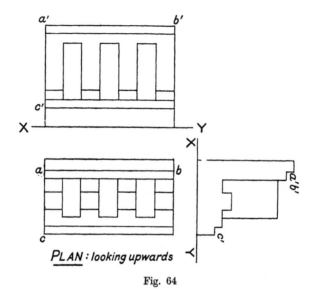

PLAN : looking upwards

Fig. 64

CHAPTER II

THE SQUARE AND OCTAGON

If a rectangle has a pair of adjacent sides equal in length, it is called a *square*.

What other definition can you suggest for a square?

In fig. 65 $ABCD$ is a rectangle in which $AB = AD$.

What else is the figure $ABCD$?
What do you know concerning the diagonals AC and BD?
What angles do AC and BD make with the sides of the figure?

A plan and elevation of the square are shown with the diagonal BD vertical and with the diagonal AC inclined to the v.p. The sides of the square are equally inclined to the ground plane; hence the sides of the figure $a'b'c'd'$ are of equal length.

Such a figure is a *rhombus*, or *lozenge*, since it is bounded by four equal sides and its angles are not right angles.

1. What can you say about the diagonals of a rhombus?
When is the plan (or elevation) of a square
   (i)   a square,
   (ii) a rhombus,
   (iii) a rectangle, which is not a square?

2. Draw three squares, the corners of a smaller being at the middle points of the sides of a next larger square. Let the largest square have 3″ sides. (You will find this a common basis of design.)

To draw a square accurately is a little difficult. We are more restricted to equality of lines and angles than in the drawing of other quadrilaterals.

We take 'squareness' very much for granted, as being a self-evident form, but the discovery of the square was a great step in geometry. The square hieroglyph represents a mat, or other woven thing, and doubtless the square arose in weaving. It is quite probable that square rooms were built for these mats.

The symmetry of the square appeals to us. In design this figure, in common with the hexagon (p. 203), lends itself to an economical arrangement with 'all-over' patterns. Most areas in buildings are rectangular and the square offers a satisfactory basis for their decoration.

Cathedral cloisters, college quadrangles and castle keeps are examples of buildings which are square in plan.

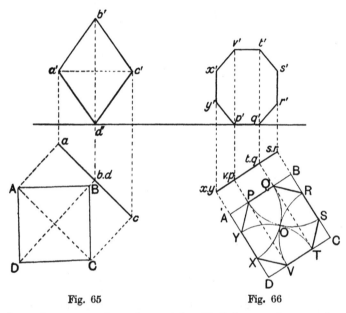

Fig. 65   Fig. 66

A *regular octagon* is a plane eight-sided figure whose angles are equal and whose sides are of equal length. Such a figure is said to be both equiangular and equilateral.

In fig. 66 *ABCD* is a square and *O* is the point of intersection of its diagonals. With the corners of the square in turn for centres and half a diagonal for radius draw arcs to cut the sides of the square in the points *P, Q, R, S, T, V, X* and *Y* as in the figure. Then *PQRSTVXY* is a regular octagon which is said to be *inscribed* in the square *ABCD*.

What is the angle of a regular octagon?

The sides XV and QR of the octagon are parallel to the diagonal AC of the square, and the sides PY and ST are parallel to the diagonal BD. AD, PV, QT and BC are parallel as also are AB, YR, XS and DC. We may also construct the octagon by inscribing a circle in the square $ABCD$ and by drawing through the points of its intersection with the diagonals AC and BD straight lines

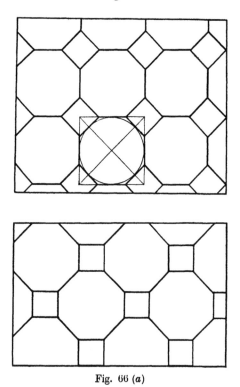

Fig. 66 (a)

PY, ST, QR and XV parallel to the diagonals. (An octagon described in this manner is shown in fig. 66 (a).)

The plan and elevation of the octagon are shown with XY or RS vertical and the plane of the octagon inclined at an angle of 30° to the v.p. In future wherever an octagon (or hexagon) occurs in this work it is considered to be a regular figure.

Octagonal forms occur somewhat rarely in objects around us. From an aesthetic point of view the figure is probably a little

uninteresting.   There may be a sense of the presence of too many
sides, resulting in a loss of simplicity.

In design the octagon occurs with the square which appears as
the interspace between the octagons placed in rows and columns.
Fig. 66 (a) shows how identical arrangements may produce
different effects from different points of view.   Sometimes
square network is used as the basis of this design, in which case
the octagons are not regular, but have four of their sides equal in
length to the side of the mesh and four sides equal to the diagonal
of the mesh.

SHADOWS OF THE SQUARE AND OCTAGON

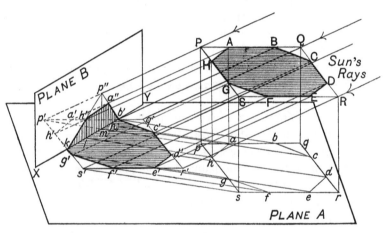

Fig. 67

The planes A and B shown in fig. 67 are at right angles to one
another and intersect in the straight line XY.

$ABCDEFGH$ is a regular octagon inscribed in a square $PQRS$,
the plane of which is parallel to the plane A and consequently at
right angles to the plane B.

$pqrs$ is the orthogonal projection of the square on the plane A
and $p'q'r's'$ is its shadow on the same plane if the plane B be
removed.

$abcdefgh$ is the orthogonal projection and $a'b'c'd'e'f'g'h'$ is the
shadow of the octagon on the plane A.

Then since the straight lines AB, BC, CD, etc., are equal in length and parallel to the plane A, it follows that their shadows on the plane A, viz. $a'b'$, $b'c'$, $c'd'$, etc., are equal and parallel to AB, BC, CD, etc.

The shadow $a'b'c'd'e'f'g'h'$ is therefore a regular octagon whose sides are equal and parallel to the corresponding sides of $ABCDEFGH$.

Now suppose the plane B to be introduced and that XY passes through b' and intersects $g'h'$, hh', pp' and aa' in the points k, l, m and n respectively.

Aaa' and Hhh' are planes at right angles to the plane A and therefore meet the plane B in straight lines $a''n$ and $h''l$ which are at right angles to XY, a'' and h'' being the points in which Aa' and Hh' meet the plane B.

$h''k$ is therefore the shadow on the plane B of that portion GH which throws a shadow $h'k$ on the plane A.

In this position the shadow cast by the octagon on the plane B is $kh''a''b'$ and on the plane A is $b'c'd'e'f'g'k$.

In fig. 68 $PQRS$ is a square the plane of which is at right angles to the plane A. $ABCDEFGH$ is a regular octagon inscribed in the square. pq is the orthogonal projection and $p'q'r's'$ is the shadow of the square on the plane A if the plane B be removed.

$pabq$ is the orthogonal projection and $a'b'c'd'e'f'g'h'$ is the shadow of the octagon on the plane A.

Now the shadow $p'q'r's'$ is a parallelogram. Since SF, ER, PA and BQ are equal and parallel to the plane A it follows that $s'f'$, $e'r'$, $p'a'$ and $b'q'$ are equal.

Also since SG, HP, RD and CQ are equal and at right angles to the plane A it follows that $s'g'$, $h'p'$, $r'd'$ and $c'q'$ are equal.

Hence it follows that $b'c'$ is equal and parallel to $f'g'$ and that $e'd'$ is equal and parallel to $h'a'$.

The shadow of the octagon is therefore an eight-sided figure whose opposite sides are equal and parallel.

Suppose the plane B to be introduced and let XY, its line of intersection with the plane A, pass through d' and cut $a'b'$ and bb' in the points k and l respectively. Also let Bb' and Cc' meet the plane B in the points b'' and c''.

Then since CD is vertical its shadow $c''d'$ on the plane B is vertical, and similarly lb'' is vertical.

In this case the shadow on the plane A is $a'kd'e'f'g'h'$ and that on the plane B is $kb''c''d'$.

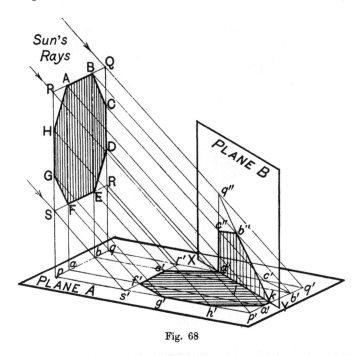

Fig. 68

Ex. A square iron vertical grille, of 3″ sides, and with bars arranged as in fig. 70, has the bottom horizontal edge 3″ from the ground. The sun, whose angle of elevation is 40°, casts the shadows of the bars on the ground. Show the shadows in plan when the vertical plane containing the rays is inclined at 60° to the plane of the grille.

SQUARE AND OCTAGONAL FORMS

The outlines of the following patterns consist of sets of parallel lines and free use should be made (except in Ex. IV) of the 45° set-square with a T-square.

Where Indian ink is not available any dark water-colour will suffice for washings.

Example I. Chequering

Reproduce fig. 69 composed of 1″ squares and fig. 71 composed of ½″ and 1″ squares.

Fig. 70, although not a correct example of chequering, may be reproduced with the sides of the larger white squares 1″ long and the rest in proportion.

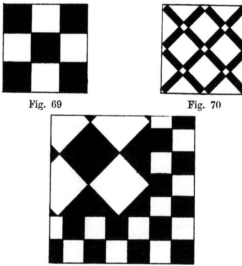

Fig. 69   Fig. 70

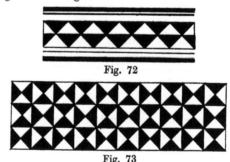

Fig. 71

Chequering is the covering of a surface with a pattern similar to that on a chessboard, in which the colour or the ornament alternates.

Example II. Interchange Ornament

Let the sides of the smallest squares in each case be ½″ and show as many repeats as are given in the figure.

Fig. 72

Fig. 73

The ornament in fig. 72 interchanges about one axis, and that in fig. 73 about more than one axis.

Example III.   Patterns

Draw the band of fig. 74 making the width of each octagon one inch and show at least two repeats.   In fig. 75 let the sides of the two equal squares which overlap symmetrically be 2″ long.

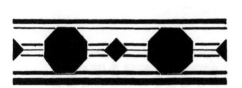

Fig. 74

Fig. 75

Example IV.   The Lozenge

Reproduce fig. 76 making the short diagonal of each lozenge 1″ in length.

Use the 60° set-square with a T-square.

The Rhombus (or Lozenge or Diamond) frequently forms the basis of design in flat decoration, being met with in wall-papers, tapestries, book-covers, glazing, etc.

Fig. 76

Example V.   The Greek Fret

Select any one fret (figs. 77–80) and work it on a net of ½ cm. squares. Notice that the breadth of the broad lines is equal to the distance between them.   Show as many repeats as are given in the figure.

As the name indicates this is specifically Greek ornament and its accommodation to square network suggests that it is of textile origin.   The development of Greek vase-painting and architecture gave rise to variations of the pattern.

The fret was seldom used in the Middle Ages but appeared again during the Renaissance.

Fig. 77

Fig. 78

Fig. 79

Fig. 80

Example VI.   Chapter-House

Draw the figure making the sides of the octagon $1\frac{1}{2}''$ long, and the rest in proportion.

The chapter-house is a hall of assembly of the chapter of a cathedral. That of Westminster was probably begun by Henry III. It stands on a smaller Norman crypt with a central pillar, and is one of the largest in England.

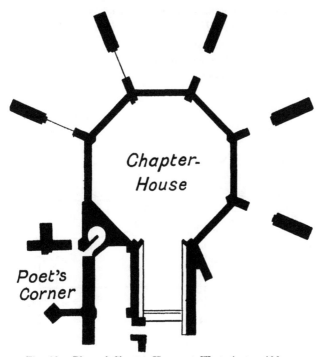

Fig. 81. Plan of Chapter-House at Westminster Abbey

The members of the convent went in solemn procession to the house. The abbot and officers took their places in stalls on the east side beneath a great crucifix, whilst the monks sat on the stone seats around, and all discussed their affairs. On the dissolution of the monasteries this chapter-house passed into the hands of the Crown, and has never been returned to the chapter. It has been used as a receptacle for state records, which have lately been removed, and the house has been completely restored.

THE CUBE: SQUARE AND OCTAGONAL
PRISMS AND PYRAMIDS

If a solid has every face a square it is called a *cube*.

Such a solid can only have six faces and at each corner there are three faces at right angles to one another and consequently each pair of opposite faces constitutes a pair of parallel planes. A cube is thus a special form of rectangular prism.

In fig. 82 *ABCDEFGH* is a cube and *AG* is one of its diagonals.

How many corners has a cube?

How many edges?   How many diagonals?

How many face diagonals?

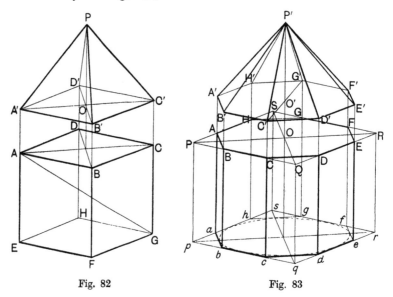

Fig. 82   Fig. 83

Let the diagonals of the face *A'B'C'D'* intersect in *O*. If a straight line *OP* be drawn from *O* at right angles to the face, and any point *P* in this straight line be joined to *A'*, *B'*, *C'* and *D'*, the solid figure *PA'B'C'D'* is called a *right square pyramid*. The point *P* is called the *vertex* of the pyramid.

The isolated pyramids found in architecture are all square in base. The Great Pyramid at Gizeh is the finest example. It is of enormous size, and seems more like a hill of stone, rising as it does from a square base of over thirteen acres, than like an architectural work.　These pyramids stood within square paved courts with walls and temples round them.　They were undoubtedly a development of the primitive grave through the mastaba (p. 194).

Obelisks are pyramidal in form, being double-angled and of one stone.　Their origin is almost as mysterious as that of the pyramids.　The earliest of the existing great obelisks belongs to a much later period than that of the Great Pyramids.　Cleopatra's Needle is one of the two obelisks which were at the entrance to the Temple of the Sun at Heliopolis.

In fig. 83 $ABCDEFGH$ is a regular octagon inscribed in a square $PQRS$.　Equal rectangles $ABba$, $BCcb$, etc., are drawn at right angles to the plane of the octagon.　The solid bounded by the rectangles and the two parallel octagonal faces $ABCDEFGH$ and $abcdefgh$ is called a *right octagonal prism*.

For a similar reason the figure $PQRSpqrs$ is a *right square prism*.

The former can clearly be obtained from a cube by chamfering any one set of four parallel edges and from a right square prism by chamfering one set.

Let PR and QS intersect in O.　If a straight line OP' be drawn at right angles to the plane of $ABCDEFGH$ and any point P' in this straight line be joined to A', B', C', D', E', F', G' and H', the solid figure $P'A'B'C'D'E'F'G'H'$ is called a *right octagonal pyramid*.

We are in future concerned only with prisms and pyramids which are *right* solids.

A paper model of the cube may be made as shown in fig. 47. To make models of the pyramids the figures $P'A'B'$, $P'B'C'$, etc., should be drawn on a piece of stiff paper with a common vertex P' and with the base of the pyramid attached to one of these figures.　The whole figure can then be cut out and fitted together, suitable flaps being left for joining adjacent edges.

In the case of the octagonal prism the rectangular faces $ABba$, $BCcb$, etc., should be drawn in a continuous rectangular strip and the octagons attached one to either side of this strip of rectangles.

Buildings of these forms occur in architecture.　The chambers of the Baths of Caracalla were octagonal.　The Pharos at Alexandria —the great lighthouse of about 280 B.C.—had an octagonal stage. An imitation of this existed once at Dover.　The octagonal

Chapter-House, of which that at Westminster is the most perfect type, was a special contribution made by the English School to the traditions of mediaeval Gothic art.   There are also buildings, octagonal in form, capped by pyramidal roofs and of the Renaissance style, of which churches at Ravenna and Pisa afford examples.

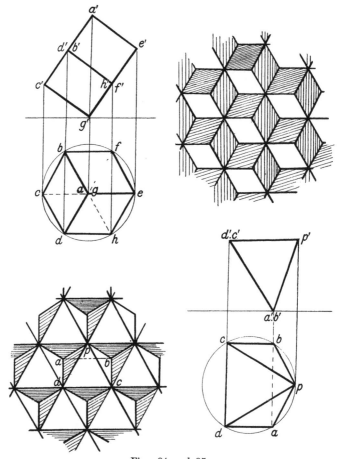

Figs. 84 and 85

The plan and elevation (fig. 84) are given of a cube *ABCDEFGH* with the diagonal *AG* at right angles to the H.P. and the edges *AE*, *BF*, *CG* and *DH* parallel to the V.P.

The edges of the cube are equally inclined to the H.P. and therefore their projections on the H.P. are equal.

The faces meeting in the point A are symmetrically arranged about the diagonal AG. Therefore the angles bae, ead, and dab are each 120°. Similarly the angles cgf, fgh and hgc are each 120°, and from symmetry gf, gh and gc bisect the angles bae, ead and dab respectively.

The plan therefore consists of three equal rhombuses or lozenges and a pattern is given based upon the repetition of these lozenges.

The plan and elevation (fig. 85) are shown of a square pyramid $PABCD$ with the edge AB in the H.P. at right angles to the V.P. and the base inclined to the H.P. In the plan the diagonals ac and bd of the rectangle $abcd$ make angles of 30° with ab. The angles cbp, bpa and pad are each 120°.

After the plan has been drawn $a'd'$ is drawn equal to ab. The height of the pyramid for a given length of ab is obtained by bisecting $a'd'$ at right angles and producing the perpendicular bisector to meet pp', parallel to ab, in the point p'.

A pattern is given based on the figure $padcb$, which is a special case arranged for this particular effect.

In fig. 86 a plan and elevation of an octagonal prism surmounted by a pyramidal 'cap' are shown. The prism rests with one octagonal face in contact with the H.P. and none of its rectangular faces are parallel to the V.P.

$abcdefgh$ is the plan of the upper and lower octagonal faces of the prism and p is the plan of the vertex of the pyramid. The straight line $h'a'g'b'f'c'e'd'$ is the elevation of the upper octagonal face of the prism and p' is the elevation of the vertex of the pyramid.

Fig. 87 shows the plan and elevation of an octagonal prism with its pyramidal cap, one of the rectangular faces of the prism lying in the H.P. and the octagonal faces being inclined to the V.P.

The straight line $habc$ is the plan of the base of the pyramid and p is the plan of its vertex. $a'b'c'd'e'f'g'$ is the elevation of the base of the pyramid and p' is the elevation of its vertex.

In both figures all necessary construction lines are clearly shown.

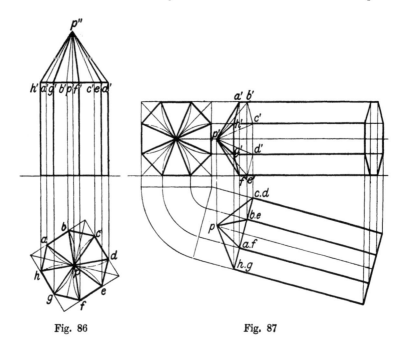

Fig. 86   Fig. 87

Ex. Draw the plan and elevation of an octagonal prism with
its pyramidal 'cap' when the prism rests with one octagonal
face in contact with the H.P.

Let the octagon be inscribed in a square the length of whose
side is 2″. Make the heights of the prism and pyramid 2″ and 1″
respectively. Let one rectangular face make an angle of 20° with
the V.P.

Ex. Draw the plan and elevation of an octagonal prism with
its pyramidal 'cap,' one of the rectangular faces of the prism
lying in the H.P. and the rectangular faces at right angles to the
H.P. making an angle of 20° with the V.P. Give also the elevation
on another V.P. at right angles to this one, the pyramid being in
front of the prism. Let the dimensions of the prism and pyramid
be the same as in the above question.

SHADOWS OF THE OCTAGONAL PRISM AND PYRAMID

In fig. 88 we have a drawing of an octagonal prism surmounted by a pyramidal cap with one face *abcd*... in contact with the plane *A*.

The direction of the sun's rays is represented by the straight lines *Aa'*, *Bb'*, *Cc'*, ..., *a'*, *b'*, *c'*, ... being points in the plane.

Aaa', *Bbb'*, *Ccc'*, ... are equal right-angled triangles in parallel planes, i.e. *aa'*, *bb'*, *cc'*, ... are equal and parallel. Hence the figures *abb'a'*, *bcc'b'*, ... are parallelograms.

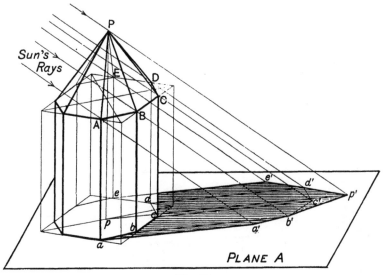

Fig. 88

The shadow cast by the prism is the same as that cast by the four faces *ABba*, *BCcb*, *CDdc* and *DEed*, all of which are at right angles to the plane *A*.

p' is the shadow of *P* the vertex of the pyramid, and in the figure *p'd'* and *p'b'* determine the limits of the shadow cast by the pyramid.

Ex. Make a similar drawing and introduce a plane *B* at right angles to the plane *A* and let the line of intersection of the two planes cut the edges *ee'* and *p'b'* of the shadow. Construct the points e'', d'' and p'', the points in which Ee', Dd' and Pp' meet the plane B, and complete the shadow as cast on the two planes.

Ex. Two cubes, the smaller standing centrally on the larger, with their edges parallel, have their sides $1''$ and $2''$ long. Show in plan the shadows on the larger cube and on the ground. The inclination of the sun's rays is 40°, and the vertical plane containing the rays is inclined at 60° to one face of the cubes.

MODELLING

The following five examples are to be modelled in clay or any other suitable medium.

Example I. A Corbel Table

Let the length of the side of the cubes be $1''$ and the rest in proportion.

Place your finished model in sunlight in a suitable position and mark lightly the edges of the shadows, and then at your desk draw an elevation, washing in the shadows.

Fig. 89

This example of a corbel table is taken from Iffley Church, near Oxford.

A corbel is a projecting stone (or timber) supporting, or seeming to support, a weight, and a row of these corbels form a corbel table. They were carved and moulded in various ways, the form of a head being very frequent.

Example II. The Square Billet Moulding

Let the length of the side of the cubes be 1″ and the rest in proportion.

This specimen of Norman moulding is found at St Augustine's, Canterbury.

Fig. 90

Example III. A Portion of a Norman Column

Let the side of the cube of which the capital is a part be 2″ long and the remaining dimensions in proportion.

Every column is divided naturally into three parts, namely, the base, shaft and capital. Fig. 91 shows the part of the shaft terminating in the necking, above which is the capital with its abacus.

5—2

In its simpler forms this capital is a cubical block of stone with its bottom corners rounded off and with a slab for an abacus placed upon it. In later Norman work the capitals are often richly moulded.

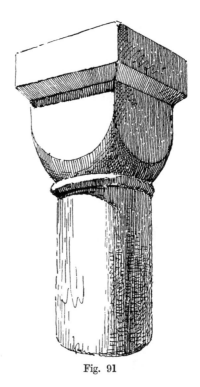

Fig. 91

Example IV. The Nail-head Moulding

Let the sides of the squares (fig. 92) be $1\frac{1}{2}''$ long and the remaining dimensions in proportion. Model at least three nail-heads.

This is a common moulding of the Norman period.

Example V. A Mullion

Let the horizontal cross-section of the mullion (fig. 93) be a regular octagon of $\frac{3}{4}''$ side. Model as much as is indicated in the figure.

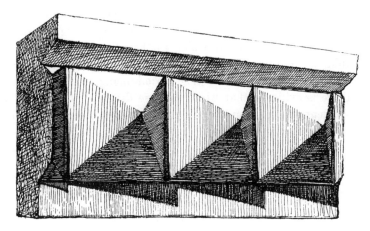

Fig. 92

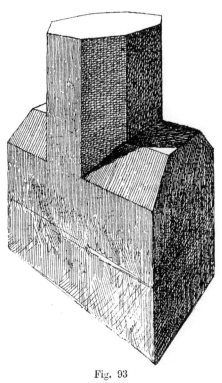

Fig. 93

A mullion is a vertical bar frequently employed in Gothic architecture to divide a window into two or more lights, and a transom is a horizontal bar which further divides it.

Mullions were introduced into our buildings during the Early English period, transoms of this period being extremely rare; but there is evidence that windows were divided by mullions in very ancient times. The transoms strengthened the mullions and were a convenience in glazing.

CHAPTER III

THE TRIANGLE AND HEXAGON

A *triangle* is a plane figure bounded by three straight lines. If two of these lines are equal in length, the figure is *isosceles,* and if all three are equal, the figure is *equilateral,* as the name implies.

The word 'isosceles' also means 'equal-sided,' but is strictly applied to the triangle, and not to any other figure.

An isosceles triangle clearly possesses one axis of symmetry and an equilateral triangle three such axes, which intersect at a point within the triangle. These three axes are three of the six axes of symmetry of the inscribed *hexagon*.

In architectural forms the isosceles triangle, with its two equal sides equally inclined to the vertical, frequently appears. The sides of the Pyramids, the openings of some Saxon lights and the gable ends of buildings afford examples.

In some cases the inclination of the equal sides to the base is governed, to a certain degree, by the purpose for which the work is intended. For example, roofs of buildings in cold countries are highly pitched with the object of quickening the displacement of snow—an object which, in warm countries, the architect need not consider. Some Gothic buildings display tall and graceful forms with a profusion of well-pitched pinnacles.

When the isosceles triangle stands on a base equal in length to its equal sides it becomes equilateral. With this proportion we have dignity and stability.

A remarkable period of our architecture has produced a number of superb churches with traceried windows, the chief curves of which are arcs of circles, which spring from the angular points of equilateral and isosceles triangles (see figs. 152–154).

In fig. 94 the plan *bac* of an equilateral triangle is shown with its elevation *a'b'c'*. The inscribed hexagon is also given in plan

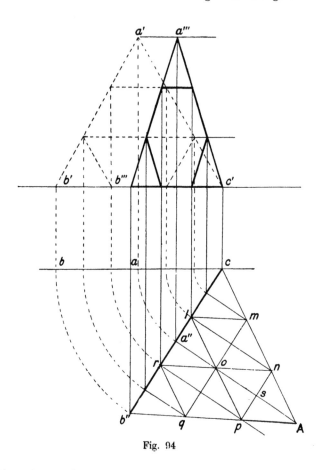

Fig. 94

and elevation, and as it appears when the triangle is rotated about *b''c* into the ground plane.

The three diagonals and three of the sides of the hexagon are each parallel to one of the sides of the triangle. There are nine equal and smaller equilateral triangles, the angles of which are 60°, and the angles of the hexagon are 2 × 60°.

The points l and r trisect the side $b''c$, and the points o and s trisect Aa''.

The equilateral triangle, the plane of which is parallel to the v.p., and the plan of which is bac, is rotated about c to the position indicated in plan by $b''a''c$. In the elevation, whilst it is rotated, the heights of the triangle and hexagon remain constant, the base decreases and each base angle increases.

From nine layers of thin paper cut out nine equal equilateral triangles, and paste them on a sheet of paper to form one larger equilateral triangle.

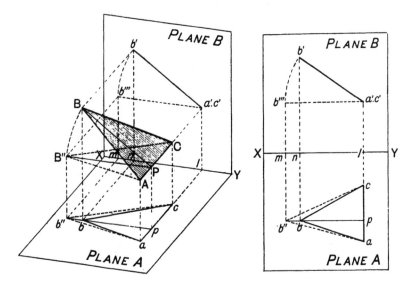

Fig. 95

The orthogonal projections of a triangle ABC are shown on two planes at right angles which intersect in the straight line XY. We may consider that on plane A to be the plan and that on plane B the elevation; or we may, by turning the figure so that plane B is in a horizontal position, consider the projection on plane B to be the plan and that on plane A to be the elevation as is shown in fig. 96.

In fig. 95 the triangle has one side AC parallel to the plane A and at right angles to the plane B. If the triangle be rotated about AC the elevation of the altitude BP does not vary in length, but its plan reaches one limit when the triangle is parallel to the plane *A* and the other limit when at right angles to it.

Ex. Experiment with a triangle and two planes at right angles cut from stiff paper. Let the shadow of the triangle in sunlight be cast on one of the planes with the rays falling perpendicularly. This may represent the orthogonal projection of the triangle on that plane. When the triangle and plane have been fixed in this position, consider the projection of the triangle on the other plane.

Give careful geometrical drawings of the plan and elevation of the triangle in its selected position.

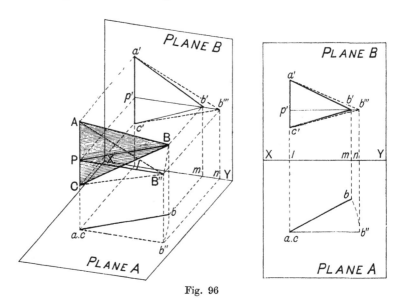

Fig. 96

Practical Work

Cut out a small triangular hole with unequal sides in a piece of stiff paper, and place the paper in sunlight so that its shadow on a plane shows an equilateral hole when the rays fall perpendicularly on the plane. Support the corners of the cut-out triangle with pins which pierce the plane at right angles at the corners of the equilateral shadow as marked on the plane, the pins representing the orthogonal projectors.

SHADOWS OF THE EQUILATERAL TRIANGLE AND HEXAGON

In fig. 97 we have an equilateral triangle ABC and its inscribed hexagon $PQRLMN$ in a vertical plane with BC parallel to the ground plane. The sun casts a shadow $a'b'c'$, etc. on the ground, the sun's rays through the angular points being represented by Aa', etc. a, p, etc. are the orthogonal projections of the points A, P, etc. on the ground plane.

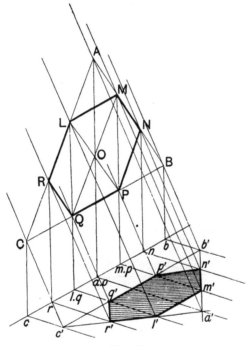

Fig. 97

The planes Aa', Ppp', etc. are thus parallel vertical planes and their horizontal traces on the ground plane, viz. aa', pp', etc., are parallel.

Which edges of the shadow are parallel to the corresponding edges of the figure?

Ex. Suppose the vertical planes containing the sun's rays to make an angle of 60° with the plane of the triangle and the sun's altitude to be 40°.　If *BC* is 3″ long, give an accurate drawing of the shadow of the hexagon.

In fig. 98 we have an equilateral triangle *ABC* and its inscribed hexagon *PQRLMN* lying in a horizontal plane and casting a shadow on the ground.　The direction of the sun's rays is indicated by the straight lines *Aa′*, *Pp′*, etc., *a′*, *p′*, etc. being points in the ground plane.　*a*, *p*, etc. are the orthogonal projections on the ground plane of the corresponding points *A*, *P*, etc.

Which edges of the shadow are parallel to the corresponding edges of the figure?

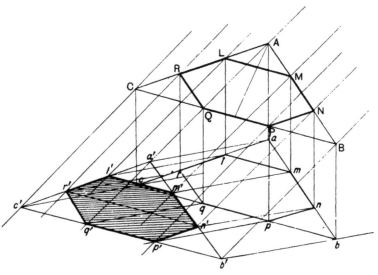

Fig. 98

Notice that the triangles *Aaa′*, *Bbb′*, etc. are equal right-angled triangles in vertical planes whose traces on the ground plane, viz. *aa′*, *bb′*, etc., are therefore parallel straight lines.

On a piece of stiff paper draw an equilateral triangle and its inscribed hexagon.　Prick a small hole through each of the vertices of the triangle and cut out the hexagon.　Let the sun's rays pass through the holes (and strike a plane) at right angles.　Hold the paper in different oblique positions, and in each case join the bright points by straight lines.　Observe the changes in the form of this orthogonal projection of the triangle and hexagon.

TRIANGULAR AND HEXAGONAL FORMS

Example I.   Patterns

Draw the two hexagonal patterns in circles of '2″ radius, filling in with Indian ink or any dark colour, and aim at accuracy and neatness.

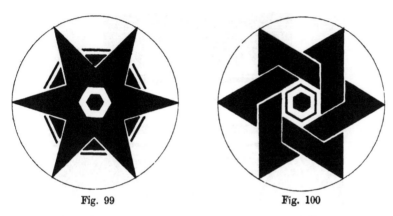

Fig. 99   Fig. 100

The former figure shows a conventional star frequently found in the decoration of tiles, ceilings, borders, etc., whilst the latter gives the interlacement of two equilateral triangular bands. This pattern may be symbolical of the Trinity.   The basis of the typical Arab patterns is formed by producing the sides of polygons and stars till they intersect in many different ways.

Example II.   Manx Ornament

This Manx ornament covers a rectangle, the short side of which is $1\frac{1}{2}″$ long. The oblique lines make angles of 60° with this side, and the bands and their interspaces are $\frac{1}{8}″$ wide.

Fig. 101

Example III.   Borders

Fig. 102, which is a flat rendering of a string course found in mediaeval work, may be drawn 1½″ wide, and fig. 103, which should be ½″ wider, is a treatment of a moulding enrichment met with in Greek design.

Use the 60° set-square with a T-square in this and the following example.

Fig. 102

Fig. 103

Example IV.   Norman Mouldings

Draw the mouldings 1½″ wide.

These characteristic Norman mouldings from Ely and Iffley are treated in the flat.   The zig-zag, or chevron, is often very profuse and elaborately decorated.   It is quite probable that zig-zag ornamentation was first copied from Oriental fabrics.   As a rule carved decoration imitated painted ornament.

Fig. 104.   Norman Moulding, Ely Cathedral

Fig. 105. Norman Moulding, Iffley, Oxon.

Example V. A Moorish Band

A Moorish band is given. You may use what proportions you think reasonable, inclining the oblique lines at 45° to the edges of the band, which is 2″ wide.

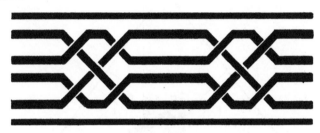

Fig. 106

Example VI. A 'Lotus' Band

Draw the 'lotus' band 2½″ wide showing at least three flowers with three wave-crests between adjoining flowers.

Fig. 107

The lotus is a plant which played an important part in the social life of the Egyptians. It was sacred to Osiris and Isis, and was the symbol of the recurring fertilization of the land by the Nile, and, in a higher sense, of immortality.

The capitals of Egyptian columns imitated the flowers and buds of this water-plant, while the shaft resembled a bound group of stalks, and the base was suggestive of the root leaves.

Example VII.   A Great Pyramid

A vertical section of the Cheops Pyramid is shown.   Reproduce it, taking care to maintain reasonable proportion in the drawing of the chambers.

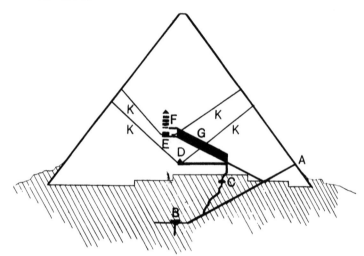

Fig. 108.   Section of the Cheops Pyramid

A, Entrance; *B*, Underground Chamber; *C*, Grotto; *D*, Queen's Chamber; *E*, King's Chamber; *F*, Construction Chambers; *G*, Grand Gallery; *K*, Air Channels

There is doubt as to the purpose of these chambers.   It is probable that when the construction of the pyramid was at the level of the King's Chamber, the position of which is shown in the figure, an earthquake caused the damage shown by the cracks in the giant beams of the roof, and that, to avoid the abandonment of the work, chambers were added above to relieve the roof of the weight of the superincumbent masonry.

For probably more than 4000 years the upper four of these

chambers were unknown. In 1765 a Mr Davison of Alexandria discovered a narrow opening in the wall of the grand gallery and after great difficulty succeeded in reaching the first chamber, and in 1837 Colonel Vyse, an Englishman, penetrated to the remaining four.

Example VIII.   Open Roofs

Sections of open roofs are given, showing the timber construction, with the names of the several parts.   Make careful drawings of them, each with a span of 4″.

In figs. 109, 110 the sections are equilateral.

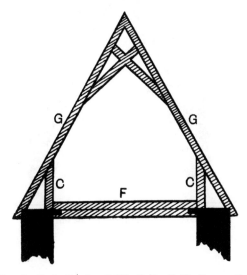

Fig. 109.   An Early Roof.   C, Side-Post; F, Tie-Beam; G, Rafter

The Greeks seem to have been the first to perfect the 'span roof,' and the Romans to have invented the principle of trussing. The latter developed timber-work, as is shown in the military bridge represented on the Trajan Column. In all Classic roofs the pitch was low since there was to be little provision against heavy falls of snow and rain.

The pitch of roofs has varied during the periods of Gothic

architecture. In Norman times roofs were occasionally steep but
in many cases the rafters meet at right angles. In Early English
examples the section is often equilateral. As the Decorated style
advanced the leading timbers of the principals were often formed
into an arch by the addition of circular braces. In Perpendicular
roofs hammer-beams were introduced, some of which are enriched
with carvings of various designs.

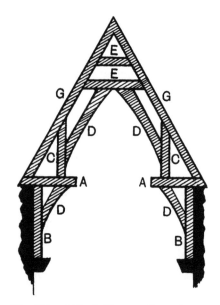

Fig. 110. A Single Hammer-Beam Roof

A, Hammer-Beam; *B*, Pendant-Post; *C*, Side-Post; *D*, Brace;
E, Collar; *G*, Rafter

TRIANGULAR AND HEXAGONAL PRISMS AND PYRAMIDS

The equilateral triangle with its inscribed hexagon has been
considered. We shall here deal with the equilateral triangular
prism and the enclosed hexagonal prism, with their respective
pyramidal caps.

In fig. 111 the altitudes AX and CZ of the triangle ABC

intersect at O. DO is at right angles to the plane of the base and is an altitude of the pyramid.

In fig. 112 P and Q trisect AB, and PT and QS are drawn parallel to CZ. PS is drawn and passes through O. VOR is drawn parallel to AB to meet AC and BC in the points V and R respectively. The angular points of the hexagon $PQRSTV$ are thus obtained.

Each prism has two equal and parallel faces, which control

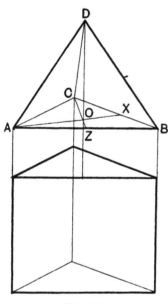

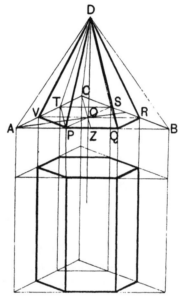

Fig. 111   Fig. 112

its form, and its remaining faces are equal rectangles. The axes of the two prisms are coincident, pass through O, and are parallel to these rectangular faces.

Hexagonal forms are found in architectural objects, such as turrets with pyramidal tops, Perpendicular shafts, etc.

The tetrahedron of which the plan and an elevation are given in fig. 113 has four equilateral triangular faces.

Give a geometrical drawing of the hexagonal star form occurring in the pattern of fig. 114 (cp. figs. 84, 85).

6—2

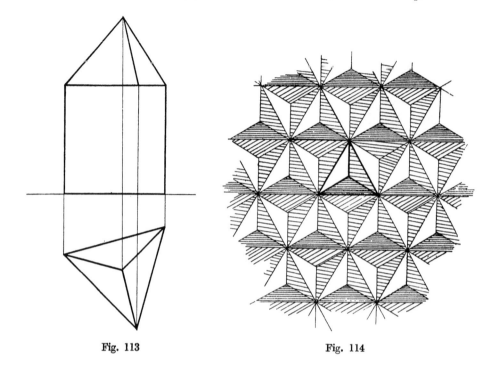

Fig. 113   Fig. 114

Practical Work

Cut out in plasticine an equilateral triangular prism. Pierce it by a knitting-needle representing its axis, and just imbed another needle along an altitude of one of the triangular faces.

What is the relative position of the needles? What is a right prism?

(i) Hold the prism obliquely so that two ends of the needles apparently coincide.

(ii, iii) Hold it in two positions so that the needles in turn appear as points.

Express these views of the prism on paper.

Test the parallelism of the edges of the rectangular faces by turning them so that they appear to coincide with the axial needle.

Chamfer the edges of the prism to form a hexagonal prism, maintaining the needles in the same position.

Experiment as above.

Cut the prism to form a pyramidal end.   Look along the axis and test the correctness of your work.

Ex.   A hexagonal prism is 2″ long and has the edges of its hexagonal faces 1″ long.   It stands on the G.P. on one of its rectangular faces, the diagonal of which is inclined to the V.P. at 45°.   Give the plan and elevation of the prism.

Ex.   The prism is now rotated about the lower horizontal edge of one hexagonal face until it again stands on the G.P.   Give the plan and elevation in the new position.

SHADOWS OF TRIANGULAR AND HEXAGONAL PRISMS AND PYRAMIDS

An equilateral triangular prism (fig. 115) is capped by a triangular pyramid *DEFG* and stands on its remaining triangular face *ABC* on the ground.   Shadows are cast by the sun partly on the ground and partly on a vertical wall (plane *B*).   Suppose the wall to be removed and the shadow entirely on the ground plane.

Dd, Ee, Ff and *Gg* represent the sun's rays, the points *d, e, f* and *g* being in the ground plane.

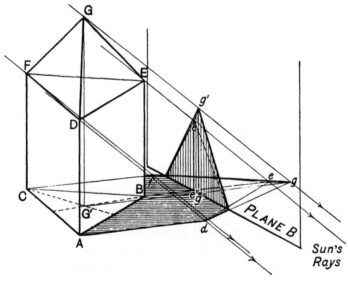

Fig. 115

DAd, EBe, FCf and *GG'g* are the typical vertical planes, the horizontal traces of which are the parallel straight lines *Ad, Be, Cf* and *G'q* respectively.

If the plane *B* be now placed in position so that the lines *dg, de, fg, fe, Be* and *G'g* intersect the ground line, the two latter in the points *e''* and *g''*, then the points *e'* and *g'* in which *Ee* and *Gg* meet the plane *B* lie vertically above *e''* and *g''*.

The outline of the shadows on the two planes is thus obtainable.

Fig. 116 shows a hexagonal prism resting on the ground on one of its hexagonal faces, *ABCDEF*. The prism is surmounted by the hexagonal pyramid *G'A'B'C'D'E'F'* and the sun casts a shadow of the whole on the ground plane.

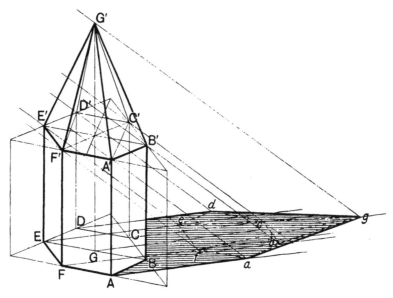

Fig. 116

Point out which lines on the ground plane are parallel.

Ex. If the lengths of *AB, AA'* and *GG'* are 1", 2" and 4" respectively, and the vertical planes containing the sun's rays are parallel to the plane *FBB'F'*, give an accurate drawing of the shadow as cast on the ground plane, the altitude of the sun being 60°

Practical Work

Cut out in plasticine an equilateral triangular prism. Arrange two planes made from stiff paper at right angles to one another and stand the prism on one rectangular face on one plane so that its shadow in sunlight on the other plane is rectangular.

What is the shadow of the triangular faces?

Stand the prism on one of its triangular faces and obtain a similar shadow.

Now let the shadows fall obliquely on the second plane and carefully mark on both planes any shadow edges which are parallel. These are important and their vanishing must be considered when the shadows are treated in perspective.

Cut your model to form a hexagonal prism and perform experiments with it as above.

Next place the model on a horizontal plane on one of its hexagonal faces.

What can you say about the shadow edges of the top face?

Carve a pyramidal end and place the model as in fig. 116. Cut out from stiff paper four triangles equal to $AA'a$. Place these in position to represent the planes $AA'a$, $BB'b$, etc., the horizontal traces of which are Aa, Bb, Cc and Dd.

Modelling

The following are a few examples to be modelled in any suitable substance. In some cases plans and elevations are given and in all one necessary measurement, from which the others should be found by means of a scale.

Example I.   A Moulding

The perspective drawing (fig. 117) gives a portion of a Norman moulding found in Westminster Hall and fig. 118 shows a section of it.

The length of AC is $1\frac{1}{2}''$.   The exterior lines in the section form part of a regular octagon.   Model about three and a half repeats.

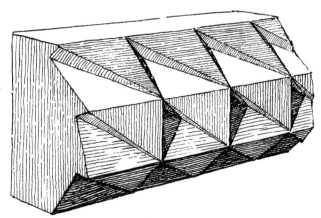

Fig. 117

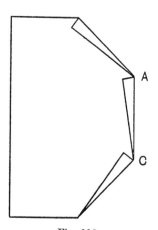

Fig. 118

Example II.   A Pattern

Two equilateral triangular bands (fig. 119) intersect, and form a hexagonal star.   Model this figure with the sides of the triangles $4''$ long and the rest in proportion.

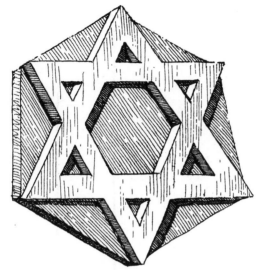

Fig. 119

Fig. 120

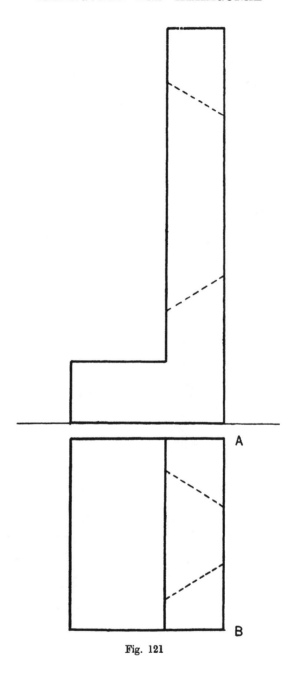

Fig. 121

Example III.   A Splayed Opening

A plan and an elevation (fig. 121) are given showing a splay of 60° of each of the four slanting sides.

Construct a scale to obtain the measurements.   The length of *AB* is 3″.

An opening is splayed by sloping its sides with the surface of the wall.   This mode of construction prevails in Gothic but is rarely used in Classic architecture.

Windows may be splayed both internally and externally.   In Norman work they are splayed internally only.

Example IV.   A Post with a Coping

A plan and an elevation (fig. 123) are given of a post, of square cross-section, surmounted by a coping the form of which suggests the interpenetration of two triangular prisms.

Make the side of the square 3″ long and the post a convenient height.

Fig. 122

Coping, or capping, is the covering course of a wall to throw off water. It often presents mouldings which characterize the period.

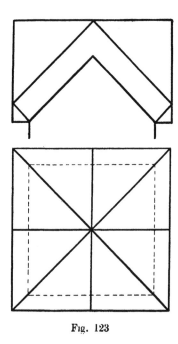

Fig. 123

Example V. A Triglyph

A front and a side elevation (fig. 125) of the triglyph are given.

Model the whole as shown, making AB 3″ in length, and give graceful proportion to your work.

The Doric frieze is divided longitudinally by triglyphs, which are projecting pieces ornamented with two whole and two half vertical channels.

In Roman examples triglyphs when placed over columns are invariably over the centre of them, but in Greek examples, at the angle of an entablature, they are placed close up to the angle and not over the centre of the column. They were usually painted a bright blue.

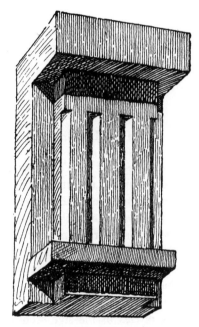

Fig. 124

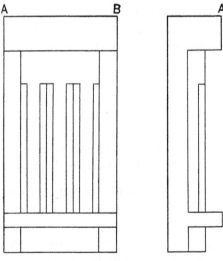

Fig. 125

CHAPTER IV

THE CIRCLE

It is extremely probable that man's knowledge of the circle dates back to remotest antiquity, and undoubtedly the fascination of the figure had no less power then than it has now. Early man may have attempted to describe a circle by hand, but it is more likely that he accidentally discovered a mechanical means of doing so. He may, for example, have observed the circular path trodden by a horse round the post to which it was tethered. The potter of old, to ornament unbaked clay, described rough circles upon it, by using his thumb and finger as a rude form of compasses.

In the Bronze Age circles of massive stones were formed to enclose burial ground. They are found in many lands. Remains exist at Stonehenge, at Avebury, and in other parts of our islands.

Coins, rings, and plates appear in various materials at all periods of history. In design the circle is usually divided into rings, each of which is decorated independently. A rosette may occur in the centre to complete the ornament. Etruscan and Assyrian shields afford early examples.

In church decoration the circle is a symbol of eternity. There are numerous patterns of circle diapers on stained glass, tiles, and hangings. The circular panel is often intricately carved, and the rose or wheel window has fantastic tracery.

Nature affords a multitude of examples of circular form, instances of which will readily occur to the student.

Let us now consider a circle from a geometrical point of view.

Suppose a point to move in a plane, so that its distance from a fixed point O in the plane is constant. Then the point traces out the bounding line of a plane figure called a *circle* of which O is the centre and the bounding line the circumference.

The straight line joining the centre to any point on the circumference is a radius.   A straight line passing through the centre and terminated at both ends by the circumference is a diameter. Every diameter divides the circle into halves or semicircles.

Open your compasses and describe a circle.   With the same centre and with the compasses less open describe a second circle. These circles are concentric and the band you have made is annular.

Cut a circle out of paper and fold it so that the two portions of the circumference coincide.

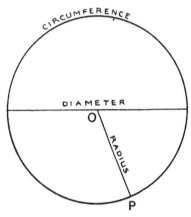
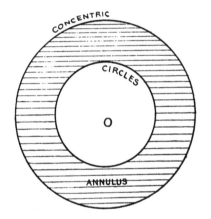

Fig. 126

What can you say about the crease?
How many axes of symmetry has a circle?

It is probable that much of the fascination of this figure is due to the fact that any diameter is such an axis, and that some of its usefulness arises from the fact that of all figures of equal area, the circle has the least perimeter.

Now draw a circle, centre O, and through O draw two diameters AOC and BOD at right angles to one another.   Through A and C draw straight lines at right angles to AC and through B and D straight lines at right angles to BD.   Let these lines meet in E, F, G and H as in fig. 127.

EF, FG, GH and *HE* are tangents to the circle, touching it at
B, C, D and *A* respectively.

What is the figure *EFGH*?

Draw the diagonals of the rectangles *HC* and *AF* and let their
points of intersection be *L* and *M*. *L* and *M* will bisect *DO* and
OB.

Find the centre *J* of the square *OBFC*. Let the straight line
through *J* parallel to *DB* cut *BF* in the point *Y*. Then *Y* is the
mid-point of *BF*.

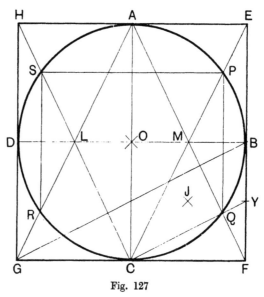

Fig. 127

Draw *CY* meeting *AF* in *Q*. *Y* may also be obtained by
drawing *CY* parallel to *GB*. Then the equal right-angled triangles
AOM and *CFY* have their sides *AO, OM* and *CF, FY* respectively
at right angles and therefore *AM* and *CY* are at right angles.

Hence, in the figure $A\hat{Q}C$ is a right angle.

This shows that *Q* is a point on the circle.

Having obtained *Q* we can quickly obtain three more points
P, S and *R* lying on the circle, as follows:

Through *Q* draw *QP* parallel to *FE* to cut *CE* in *P*.

Through *P* draw *PS* parallel to *EH* to cut *CH* in *S*.

Through S draw SR parallel to HG to cut AG in R.

The rectangle $PQRS$ has its sides parallel to the sides of the square $EFGH$.

Let the plane of the circle be inclined to the H.P. with the diameter DB horizontal and let ac be the orthogonal projection of the diameter AC. The projection of the circle on the H.P. will be a curve as shown in fig. 128. This curve is an ellipse, of which bd and ac are the major and minor axes respectively.

The square $EFGH$ projects into a rectangle $efgh$ which circumscribes the ellipse, and points p, q, r and s may be found on the ellipse by the same construction as was used to determine P, Q,

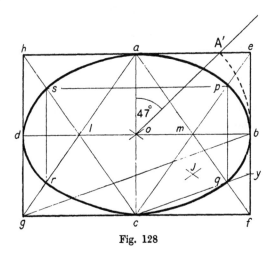

Fig. 128

R and S for the circle. Thus eight points on the ellipse may easily be found and a freehand drawing of the curve then made.

The plan of the *horizontal diameter* of the circle is always equal to the diameter of the circle. The length of the minor axis of the ellipse can easily be found when the angle of inclination of the plane of the circle to the H.P. is known.

In the figure drawn this angle was taken to be 47°. Draw db equal to DB and through o the mid-point of db draw aoc at right angles to db. Make $a\hat{o}A'$ equal to 47°.

Cut off oA' equal to ob. Through A' draw hae at right angles to oa.

This determines the point a, for oa is the plan of OA' inclined at an angle of 47° to the H.P.

As the circle is rotated about the horizontal diameter DB its plan varies.

When the plane of the circle is parallel to the H.P. its plan is an equal circle, so we may look upon this circle as the limiting form of the ellipse when its axes are of equal length.

When the plane of the circle is perpendicular to the H.P. its plan is a straight line. This is the limiting form of the ellipse when its minor axis is zero.

Practical Work

1. From layers of thin paper cut out several equal semi-circular tiles with rectangular tops. Let the length of the diameter be 1″ and the other side of the rectangle ¾″. Paste these on stiff paper to tile an area 8″ by 4″.

2. Draw the plan of a circle whose diameter is 3″ long when the plane of the circle is inclined,

          (i)   at an angle of 30°,

          (ii) at an angle of 60°

to the H.P.

SHADOWS OF CIRCLES

In fig. 129 a drawing is given of a circle enclosed in a square $ABCD$ and placed in sunlight so as to cast a shadow on the ground. The plane of the circle is supposed to be parallel to the ground so we know that the shadow $a'b'c'd'$ of the square is an equal square whose edges are parallel to the corresponding edges of the square $ABCD$.

The shadow of the circle is therefore an equal circle inscribed in the square $a'b'c'd'$.

In fig. 130 the plane of the circle and its enclosing square $ABCD$ is supposed vertical and we take AB parallel to the ground. The shadow $a'b'c'd'$ of the square on the ground is a parallelogram and the shadow of the circle is an ellipse touching the parallelogram at the middle points of its sides.

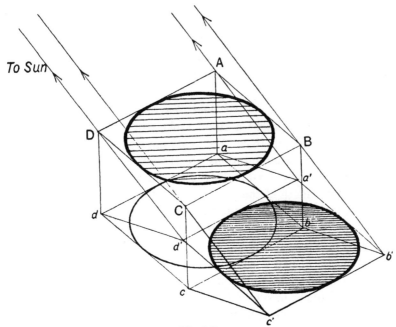

To Sun

Fig. 129

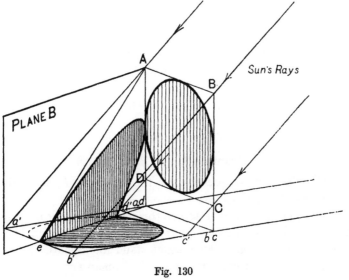

Sun's Rays

PLANE B

Fig. 130

7—2

A vertical plane B is introduced passing through AD and the point e in which the shadow of the circle touches $a'b'$. The shadow of the circle on the plane B is a part of an ellipse which touches AD at its middle point and Ae at e, and passes through the point in which ed again cuts the edge of the shadow of the circle on the H.P.

Practical Work

1. Hold in sunlight a circular piece of stiff paper with the two sides not illuminated. Define its position with regard to the sun's rays. In what positions are the shadows on a horizontal plane greatest and least? In the former case find by geometry the greatest length of this shadow when the diameter of the circle and the inclination of the sun's rays are given.

When is the shadow circular? State the two positions.

2. On the ends of an uncut pencil fix symmetrically two equal circles of paper, say of 2″ diameter, the axis of the pencil being at right angles to the planes of the circles.

Cast shadows in sunlight on any plane so that

  (a)   the shadows have no curves,
  (b)   the shadows of the two circles coincide,
  (c)   the shadow is composed of two ellipses touching one another,
  (d)   the shadows are both circles.

Ex. Show in plan only the complete shadows of the above circles and pencil when the elevation of the sun is 75°, and when the vertical plane containing the rays is inclined at 30° to the vertical plane containing the pencil, which is horizontal.

CIRCULAR FORMS

Example I.   S. P. Q. R.

With ruler and compasses draw the letters S, P, Q, R about 2″ high and of any thickness.

It is not usual to form letters in this harsh geometrical manner, since an artist is allowed liberty in displaying originality in shape and in spacing. These letters stand for 'Senatus Populusque Romanus' and frequently appear in Roman art.

S.P.Q.R.

Fig. 131

Example II. Bands

Copy these two bands, making the centres of the circles 1″ apart and the rest of the measurements in proportion.

Fig. 132   Fig. 133

Example III. Imbrication

Let the centres of the semicircular tiles be 1½″ apart, and show sufficient to cover a rectangle 6″ × 3″.

The fir cone, the hop, the bark of the Chile pine, the scales of fishes and the feathers of birds show this arrangement of overlapping scales, and since roof-tiles are placed in this way to carry off the rain the term 'imbrication' is used.

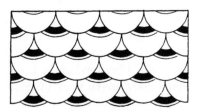

Fig. 134

Roofs of Doric and Ionic buildings were covered with tiles, which were often wrought in marble and adjusted with amazing precision. Chinese roofs, which are sometimes covered with elaborate tiles, show signs of Greek origin.

Example **IV.** Trefoils

The dotted arcs of circles which determine the position of O have for radius a length equal to $O'O''$ in fig. 135 and a length less than $O'O''$ in fig. 136.   In each case let $O'O''$ be $1\frac{1}{2}''$ long.

The trefoil in heraldry represents the clover leaf, and is always furnished with a stalk.   In architecture it is a three-lobed aperture, and is frequently decorated in a simple manner.

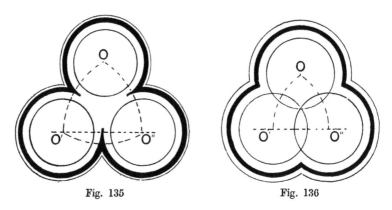

Fig. 135   Fig. 136

Example **V.** Braided Ornament

In your drawing make $PQRS$ (fig. 137) $1''$ square, and the width of the bands in proportion.   Decide which are the structural lines, and then you can more easily insert the concentric and intersecting arcs which mostly compose the figure.

This is a form of braided and knotted decoration which was practised during Saxon times in book decoration and in stone carving.   It is of Byzantine origin.   The same type of ornamentation was known all over Christendom in the eighth and ninth centuries, and in Rome itself much work of this sort is found.

Example **VI.** A Cairene Dome

A section (fig. 138) showing the form of a Cairene dome is given.   The construction is as follows:

With centre O draw the circle BCQ and let DQ be its vertical diameter.   Take a point P on OQ such that $PQ = \frac{1}{4}OQ$, and

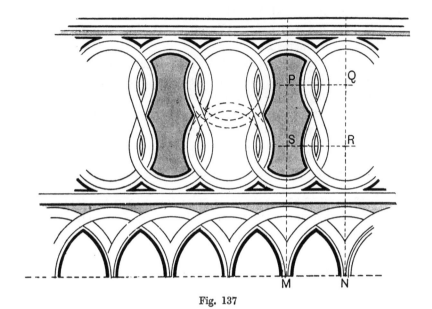

Fig. 137

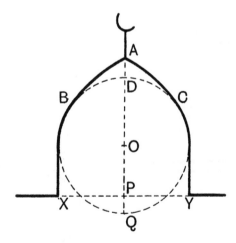

Fig. 138. The Form of a Cairene Dome

through P draw a horizontal line XY cutting the vertical tangents to the circle in X and Y. These points are the centres of the circular arcs BA and CA, BOY and COX being straight lines.

Make the diameter DQ 3″ long.

From the domed tombs of Cairo we get the type of the Renaissance dome. It is quite probable that the domes of St Mark's, Venice, were suggested by Arab domes of this kind. There is nothing barbaric in Cairene tombs, indeed the later examples display extraordinary beauty.

Example VII.   Sections of Roman Mouldings

These sections are based on circular forms, and the centres of the arcs are shown in the figures. The radii of the Ovolo and Cavetto should be 1″ long, and those of the Torus, and Cyma

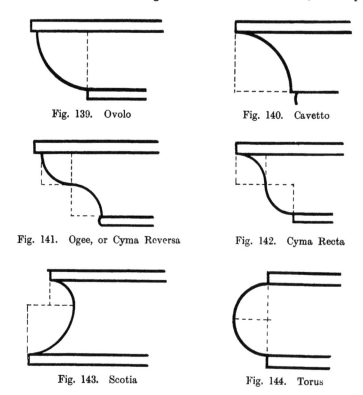

Fig. 139.   Ovolo

Fig. 140.   Cavetto

Fig. 141.   Ogee, or Cyma Reversa

Fig. 142.   Cyma Recta

Fig. 143.   Scotia

Fig. 144.   Torus

Reversa and Recta should be $\frac{1}{2}''$ long. Make the radii of the arcs of the Scotia $\frac{3}{8}''$ and $\frac{3}{4}''$ long.

The Greeks with their usual refinement of taste developed the art of moulding to a high degree of perfection. They rejected the circular forms and favoured those which approximated to conic sections. To the Romans, with their engineering instincts and practical application of their arts, the use of first principles and simple constructions appealed more strongly, and thus their curves are frequently composed of compass-drawn arcs.

With the Greeks the Ovolo in section resembles the outline of an egg. The Cavetto, as the name implies, is hollow. As a general rule the lines of the ornament on the moulding correspond to the profile of the moulding itself. The Cyma Recta and Cyma Reversa are two interesting wave forms, the latter giving the half of the Ogee arch. The Scotia which is common in the bases of Roman columns is entirely concave, and casts a deep shadow, useful in architectural design. The Torus is large and convex, and generally the lowest of a series of mouldings.

Example VIII.　Arches

The positions of the centres are shown in the figures and the lengths of the radii are given below:

Figure	Radius
145	$1\frac{1}{2}''$
146	$2\frac{1}{2}''$
147	$2\frac{1}{4}''$
148	$2\frac{1}{2}''$ and $\frac{1}{4}''$
149	$1''$ and $1\frac{1}{2}''$

Arches are found in Egypt dating from dynastic times. The true masonry arch appeared later and seems to have developed in Egypt some 2000 years after the brick vault. From the recent discovery of arches at the Piraeus it is probable that they were in general use among the Greeks before their introduction to Italy, at which time the general form was semicircular. The pointed arch used by Byzantine builders was typical of the Arabian style, and by the eleventh century was distributed over Europe and in the next century reached England.

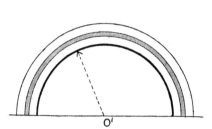

Fig. 145.   Norman Arch

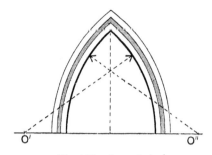

Fig. 146.   Lancet Arch

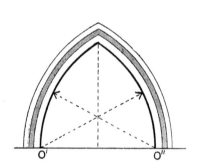

Fig. 147.   Equilateral Arch

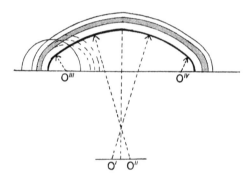

Fig. 148.   Tudor Arch

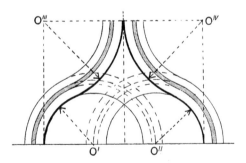

Fig. 149.   Ogee Arch

Example IX.   The Quatrefoil and its Half

The four leaves of this figure are arcs of circles, the centres of which are at the points P, Q, R and S, the middle points of the sides of a 2″ square. In fig. 151 half the quatrefoil is seen with the same dimensions.

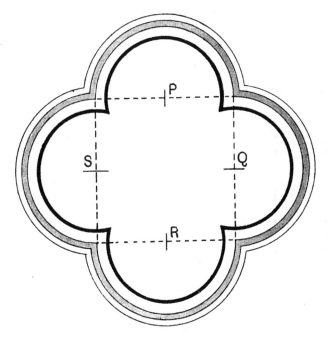

Fig. 150

The quatrefoil was a favourite feature of Saxon work, so much so that it may be considered a Saxon contribution to European art. It seems to have been adopted for windows by the eleventh century.

The half-quatrefoil arch also made an early appearance in Anglo-Saxon work.

Trefoil arches appear on the Bayeux Tapestry, which is almost certainly an English work, and also in Ely and Lincoln Cathedrals.

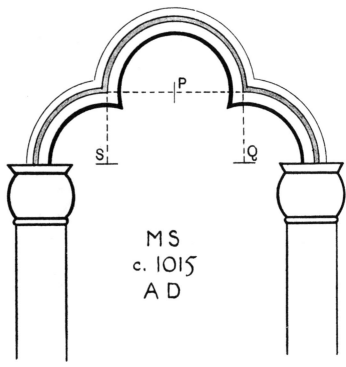

Fig. 151

Example X.   Decorated Tracery

These three arches are equilateral as are also most of their subdivisions. Carefully decide which are the structural lines before you proceed with the inking of your figures. Let the arches span a length of 3″.

Bar tracery probably originated from interlacing arches such as are found in the wall arcading at Castle Rising, and in the abbey at Romsey.

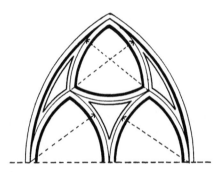

Fig. 152.   Capel St Mary Church, Suffolk

Fig. 153.   Northfleet Church, Kent

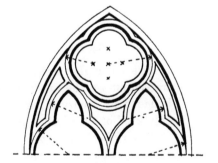

Fig. 154.   Northfleet Church, Kent

THE SPHERE, CONE, CYLINDER AND RING

If a point moves so that its distance from a fixed point is always the same, it will trace out the surface of a *sphere*. The fixed point is the centre and any straight line through it terminated by the surface is a diameter.

The orthogonal projection of the figure is simple, since it is symmetrical about any diameter, but the perspective projection is not so. For these purposes the length of a diameter and its position in space will be considered.

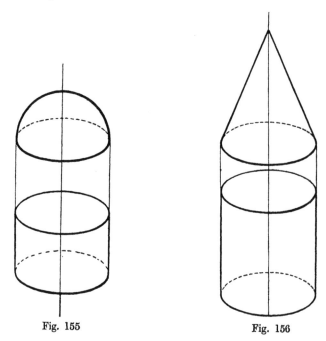

Fig. 155   Fig. 156

If a rectangle rotates about one of its sides as axis the figure traced out by the other sides is a *right circular cylinder*. It is bounded by a curved surface and two equal circles. This is the only kind of cylinder we are considering.

The *right circular cone* is traced out by a right-angled triangle rotating about one of the sides containing the right angle. It is bounded by a curved surface and a circle. We are concerned only with this form of cone.

The *ring* of model drawing is merely a hollow cylinder of short length (fig. 157).

In architecture the hemisphere is more frequently met with than the complete sphere. The latter is usually placed in conspicuous places, being symbolical of power.

The hemispherical dome has appeared in all the ages of man, from the domical tombs of Egypt to the superb Renaissance domes of Italy.

The apse, or termination to the choir or aisle of a basilica, was often circular and capped by a half-dome, or quarter-sphere. It was probably of Eastern origin, for the half-dome must have come from the land of domes. It appears to have been known to the Greeks.

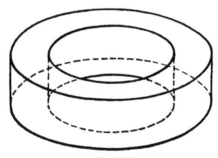

Fig. 157

In fig. 155 a hemisphere and cylinder are shown with circles of equal radii. They suggest a domical roof surmounting a drum. This form of building is met with even in very early times. The roof of St Paul's Cathedral shows this method of termination.

Fig. 156 shows a cone and cylinder with circles of equal radii and suggests a method of terminating a round tower.

Practical Work

The Sphere

[These models should be used for the practical work on shadows.]

1. Model a sphere of 2″ diameter, and divide it into hemispheres. Arrange these in the positions indicated in figs. 161, 162 and give the plans and elevations to scale.

2. Divide one of the hemispheres into halves and place these as shown in figs. 159, 160, giving plans and elevations to scale.

The Cone

3. Model a cone of 2″ altitude and 2″ diameter of base circle. Place the cone in the positions indicated in figs. 164, 165 and in the latter case give a plan and elevation. The curve may be projected by the method shown in figs. 127, 128, Part I.

4. Truncate the cone and perform the same operations for figs. 166, 167.

The Cylinder and Ring

[Figs. 174 and 176 show the ring in plan and elevation.]

5. Model a cylinder of 2″ diameter and $\frac{1}{2}$″ axis and place it in the positions shown in figs. 171 and 172. Halve the cylinder for fig. 170 and hollow one-half for figs. 175 and 177.

Give plans and elevations to scale of each of the above.

Ex. Figs. 158, 163, 168 and 173 show plans and elevations of groups of solids. Give elevations on v.p.s inclined in each case at 30° to the given v.p.s.

What solid is shown in plan and elevation in fig. 169?

Ex. Give the plan and elevation of the square pillar surmounted by a sphere as shown in fig. 92, Part II. The radius of the sphere is 1″, and the side of the pillar is $1\frac{1}{2}$″ long. The projecting square moulding is $\frac{1}{4}$″ in section, and one horizontal diagonal of the pillar is inclined to the v.p. at 60°.

Ex. Two equal truncated cones are fixed together at their smaller circular faces in a manner suggested in the double-cone moulding of fig. 192. The lengths of the radii of the circles are 1″ and 2″, and the length of the axis of each cone is $1\frac{1}{2}$″. Their common axis is horizontal and inclined to the v.p. at 60°. Show them in plan and elevation, projecting the circles by the method of fig. 128.

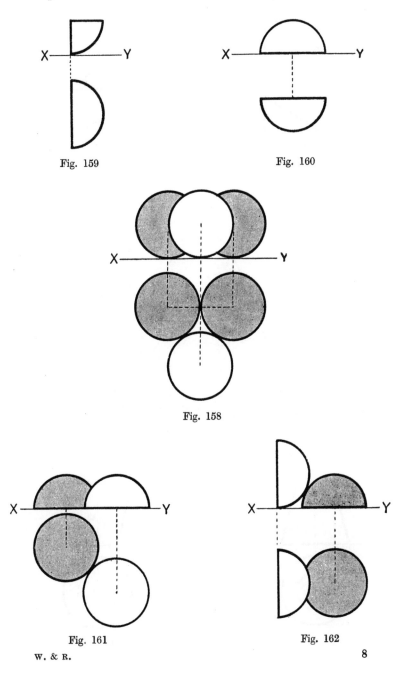

Fig. 159

Fig. 160

Fig. 158

Fig. 161

Fig. 162

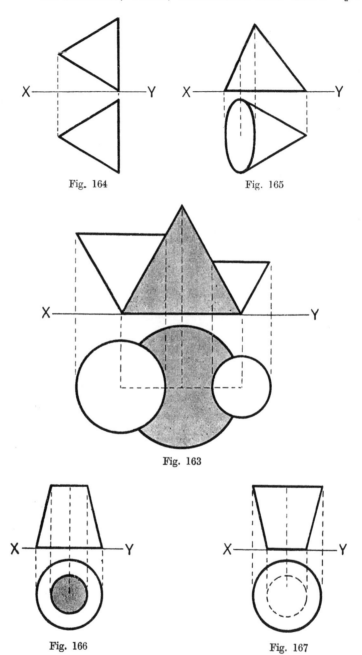

Fig. 164

Fig. 165

Fig. 163

Fig. 166

Fig. 167

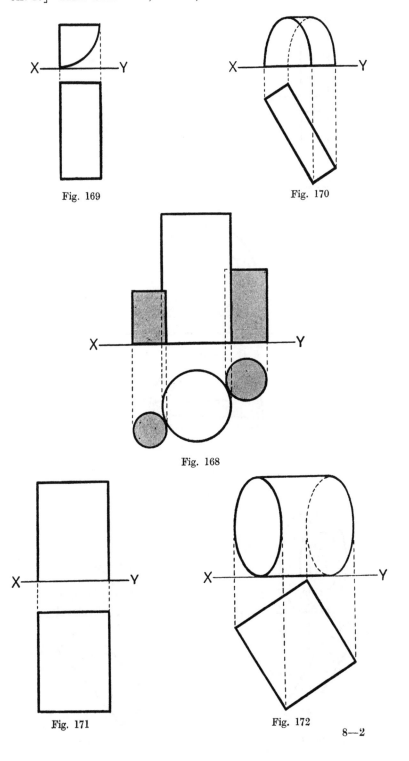

Fig. 169

Fig. 170

Fig. 168

Fig. 171

Fig. 172

8—2

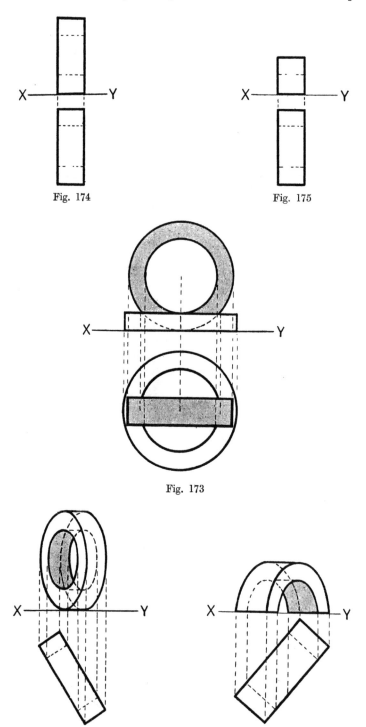

Fig. 174

Fig. 175

Fig. 173

Fig. 176

Fig. 177

SHADOWS OF THE SPHERE, CONE, AND CYLINDER

At the ends of any straight support XY fix at right angles to its length two equal circles AB and CD of stiff paper. Place the circles in the position indicated in the figure, and let the sun's rays cast a shadow ab of the upper circle AB on a plane surface. Trace a line round this shadow and compare its shape and size with that of the circle CD (or AB) by placing the circle on the shadow.

Replace the support in its original position and on the end X fix a sphere of plasticine of the same diameter as AB. Trace out

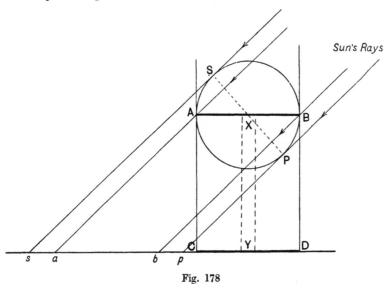

Fig. 178

the shadow sp of the sphere and compare it with the shadow of the circle. [Refer to figs. 179 and 181.]

In fig. 179 we have the shadow of a sphere cast on a plane by the sun's rays. We see that it is the same as that of the central circular section of the sphere which is at right angles to the sun's rays. The square enclosing this section is represented in the figure by $ABCD$, and $abcd$ is its orthogonal projection on the plane. The sides AB and DC are taken for simplicity in the vertical plane containing the sun's rays.

The shadow of the square is thus a rectangle $a'b'c'd'$ and that of the sphere is the ellipse which touches the sides of the figure $a'b'c'd'$ at their middle points, and which may be drawn by the method of fig. 128.

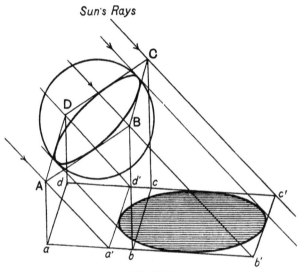

Fig. 179

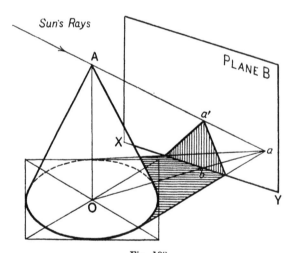

Fig. 180

We have shown in fig. 180 the shadow of a cone on two planes at right angles to one another. The cone has its base in contact with one of the planes and the shadow of the vertex *A* on the plane is *a*. The shadow of the cone on this plane is obtained by drawing tangents to the base circle from the point *a*.

If *Aa* meets the second plane *B* in the point *a'*, then *a'* is the shadow of *A* on the plane *B*, and the shadow on the two planes is easily completed.

If *O* is the centre of the base circle and *Oa* meets *XY* the line of intersection of the two planes in the point *b*, what is the direction of *ba'*?

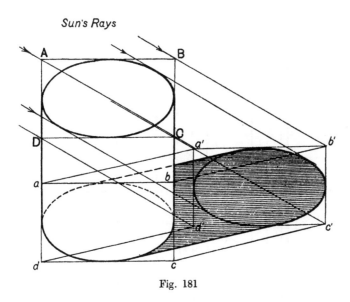

Fig. 181

Fig. 181 shows the shadow cast by a cylinder on a plane, one circular face of the cylinder resting on the plane. *ABCD* is a square enclosing the upper circular face of the cylinder and *abcd* is its orthogonal projection on the plane. Thus *abcd* encloses the lower circular face. *a'b'c'd'* the shadow of *ABCD* on the plane is also a square, and the shadow of the upper face would be the circle enclosed by this square. To complete the edges of the shadow of the cylinder we draw straight lines touching both its circle of contact with the plane and this latter circle.

Ex. A sphere rests in contact with a cylinder on the H.P.
The radii of the sphere and of the circular faces of the cylinder, on
one of which it rests, are each 1″ long and the axis of the cylinder
is 2″ long. The elevation of the sun is 60° and the vertical plane
containing the sun's rays is inclined at 45° to the plane in which
all the centres lie. Show in plan only, the complete shadows on
the ground of the two objects.

Fig. 182 shows a plan and elevation of a circular shaft on
which are marked twelve straight lines parallel to its axis and

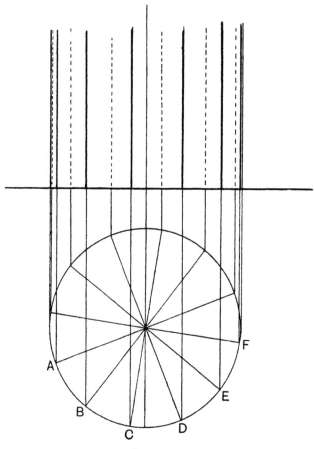

Fig. 182

placed at equal distances round its circumference. The points
A, *B*, *C*, etc. are obtained on the circular plan by drawing
diameters making angles of 30° with one another.

This figure is suggestive of the flutings of columns. The
earliest show only slight flutings, but later their sections have a
variety of depths and shapes. The Greek Doric column was
generally divided into twenty flutes in order to allow an arris to
appear under the most projecting points of the abacus above.

Ex. Draw a similar figure making the diameter of the circle
3″ long, and showing twenty flutings and an abacus.

If a circle is inclined to a plane one diameter can be drawn
which is parallel to the plane, and the lengths of this diameter
and of chords which are parallel to it are unaltered by orthogonal
projection on the plane. Moreover, the diameter which bisects
this set of chords at right angles makes with the plane the angle
of inclination of the circle with the plane. When this angle is
known the foreshortened length of this latter diameter may be
drawn in the plan (or elevation) of the circle. The unaltered
lengths of the set of chords which it bisects (these are still bisected
at right angles by it in the plan) may then be set out each in its
own proper position across the diameter, and the curve completed
by freehand drawing. It is usually sufficient to divide into six
or eight equal parts a diameter of the circle to be projected and
to transfer the lengths of the chords, which pass through the
points of division at right angles to the diameter, to the corresponding projections of the points of division.

Modelling

The following are a few examples to be modelled in any suitable
substance. In some cases plans and elevations are given and in
all one necessary measurement, from which the others should be
found by means of a scale.

Example I.   Strung Coin Moulding

Let the diameter of each coin (fig. 183) be 2″ long and the remaining measurements in proportion.

Model about three and a half repeats.

A section of one of the coins is shown in fig. 183 (a).

Fig. 183

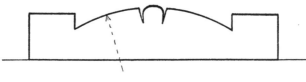

Fig. 183 (a)

Example II. Guilloche Moulding

A cross-section of a band is shown. Let its width be $\frac{3}{4}''$ and show about three repeats.

This ornament is found on Assyrian and Greek monuments, two or more rows being sometimes interlaced. The design is probably suggested by the intertwining of ropes round circular pins, as is seen on a beautifully carved mace-head in the British Museum. In plastic work the bands were frequently fluted or channelled, and in flat treatment the interlacing bands are distinguished from each other by shading or colour.

Fig. 184

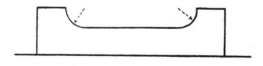

Fig. 185

Example III. Guttae

A plan looking upwards and an end elevation are given. The centres of the base circles are 1″ apart. Draw a scale to obtain the remaining measurements.

These guttae or 'drops,' which appear in the Doric entablature, may represent wooden pins, since they hang beneath the sloping mutules and below the triglyphs. They were sometimes cylindrical and not conical as shown here.

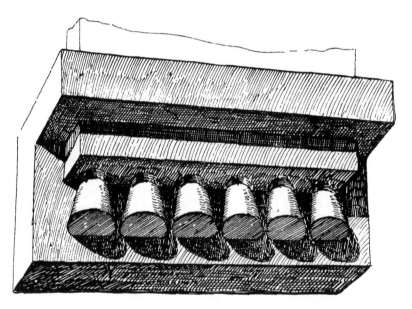

Fig. 186

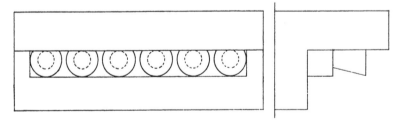

Fig. 187

Example IV. Ovolo Moulding

A cross-section is given. The radius of the quarter-circle is
1½″ long (see p. 105).

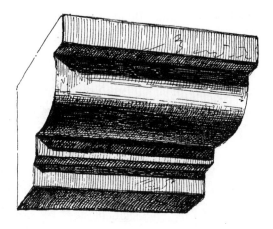

Fig. 188

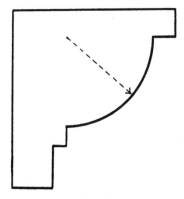

Fig. 189

Example V.   Pellet Moulding

A portion of a circular moulding is shown, and a section through the centre of one of the pellets is also given.   Let the pellets be hemispherical of 1″ radius.

Pellet, Double-Cone and Billet mouldings are interesting features of Norman work.

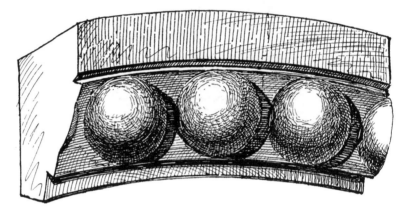

Fig. 190

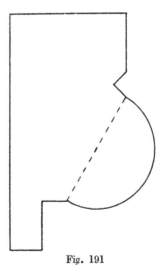

Fig. 191

Example VI. Double-Cone Moulding

Let the diameter of the base of a cone be $1\frac{1}{2}''$ long. Two elevations are given and by aid of a scale the remaining measurements are to be determined.

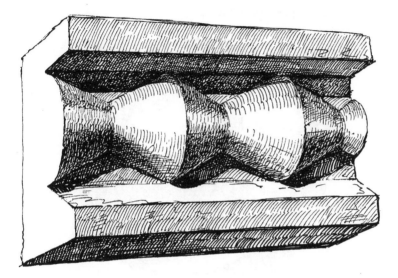

Fig. 192

This example is taken from the church at Stoneleigh in Warwickshire.

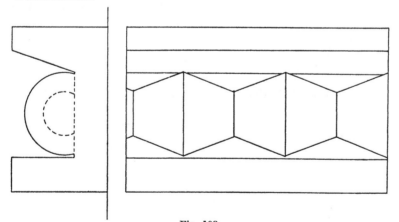

Fig. 193

Example VII.   Ball-flower Ornament

Let the diameter of the flower be 3″ long.   Model it on a slab and take a little liberty with the design in your attempt to produce an effective piece of ornament.

Fig. 194

This ornament resembles a ball placed in a flower, and is generally characteristic of the decorated style of the fourteenth century.

One theory as to its origin is that it represents a pomegranate, and was introduced out of compliment to Queen Eleanor of Castile.   In all probability, however, it is of Eastern origin.

PART II

CHAPTER V

RECTANGLES

PERSPECTIVE PROJECTION

The drawings of Part I have been either simple plans or elevations of the objects under consideration. The plan and elevation—though convenient representations of the object on plane surfaces, for they can be accurately measured to scale—are not the projections of the object as the eye would see it, unless the eye be supposed to be moved opposite each point of it in succession.

Imagine you are looking through a window at any point A, your eye being fixed, and suppose a straight line AE drawn to your eye, E, from the point. If the straight line AE meet the plane of the window in a', then a' is called the *perspective projection* on the plane of the point A. If b' is the perspective projection of some other point B, then the straight line $a'b'$ on the plane of the window is the perspective projection of the straight line AB.

In practice we imagine the plane upon which our perspective projection is made to be at right angles to the line of our direct vision, or *central visual ray*, and the plane is called the *picture plane*, denoted by P.P., and meets the H.P. in the *picture line* or *ground line*.

The central visual ray, denoted by C.V.R., meets the picture plane in the *centre of vision*, which is denoted by C.V.

The line of intersection of the horizontal plane through the eye with the P.P., *whether the* P.P. *be oblique or vertical*, is the *eye-line* or horizon. When the C.V.R. is horizontal the C.V. lies on this line, otherwise it does not.

In the figures the perspective projection $a'b'c'd'$ of a rectangle $ABCD$ lying on the ground is shown as intercepted on a window

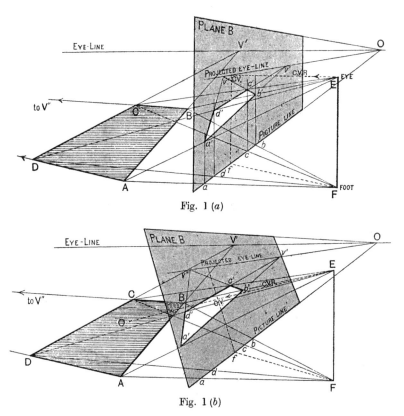

Fig. 1 (*a*)

Fig. 1 (*b*)

pane, represented by the plane B, the C.V.R. being here supposed at right angles to the window pane and indicated in the figures by the dotted line from E. The points a', b', c' and d' are the points on the window pane through which the straight lines EA, EB, EC and ED pass. F is the foot of the spectator and FA, FB, FC and FD are straight lines in the H.P. cutting the picture line in the points a, b, c and d.

In fig. 1 (*a*) the C.V.R. is horizontal so the picture plane is vertical, but in fig. 1 (*b*) the C.V.R. is not horizontal and thus the picture plane is oblique. In the latter case the C.V.R. is drawn to some convenient central point *O* of the object, here the point of intersection of the diagonals *AC* and *BD* of the rectangle.

Unless otherwise stated it will be assumed in future that the C.V.R. is horizontal, i.e. that the picture plane is vertical. When we view above or below our eye-level a single object, an architectural detail or some portion of a building, where such are observed as things apart and not as parts of a whole, our C.V.R. is no longer horizontal and our picture plane is necessarily oblique.

We are about to discuss a geometrical method of representing on paper the result which has been obtained on the window. All perspective drawings from the object, whatever method we may adopt, are really attempts to portray the object as the eye sees it, and accurate methods are difficult. It is thus convenient to establish uniform laws of perspective projection. The further study of figs. 1 (*a*) and 1 (*b*) should be postponed until the laws have been deduced.

In fig. 2 *PP'* and *BC* are the lines of intersection of the plane of the paper with the P.P. and a plane parallel to the P.P. respectively. *AB* and *DC* are equal lengths measured along the line of intersection *BC*, and *ab* and *dc* are their projections, *E* being the position of the eye.

By a theorem in Geometry, if *AB* is equal to *DC* then *ab* is equal to *dc*.

If then any number of equal straight lines lie in the same plane parallel to the P.P. their projections on the P.P. are equal.

The length of a straight line as apparent to the spectator is not equal to its projection on the P.P., but is measured by the *angle of sight*, i.e. the angle subtended by the straight line at the eye. Here *CD appears* shorter than *AB*, for the angle *CED* is less than the angle *AEB*, but *CD* and *AB* have equal projections on the P.P.

Suppose the plane which contains *AB* and *DC* and which is parallel to the P.P. to recede from the P.P., but remain parallel to it, whilst *A* and *B* move along straight lines at right angles to

9—2

the P.P. Then corresponding to the positions $A'B'$, $A''B''$, ... of AB we have the projections $a'b'$, ...

As AD recedes from the P.P. how does its projection change? How does the angle of sight change?

If AB recedes to an infinite distance what is the angle of sight? What is the projection of AB on the P.P. and where is it situated?

The angle of sight for clear vision is limited in size to about 60°, and if the object is too near the eye the image is blurred. In making a drawing this is a point to be noticed.

In photographic work with a camera the field of view is limited in order to avoid blurring at the edges of the picture. Here the

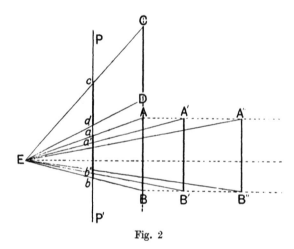

Fig. 2

lens of the camera takes the place of the eye and the angle of the lens corresponds to the angle of sight. In many cameras the lens slides up or down in a plane parallel to the photographic plate, the latter being usually retained in a vertical position. The photograph obtained in this manner is a projection on a vertical P.P. If however the plate be tilted, as would be necessary in photographing an aeroplane in flight or buildings as seen from an aeroplane, the picture obtained is a projection on an oblique P.P.

Place two rectangular cards $AA'B'B$ and $CC'D'D$ on a table near a window so that the plane of $AA'B'B$ is vertical, with BB'

resting on the table at right angles to the plane of the window,
and so that the plane of $CC'D'D$ is horizontal, with CC' at right
angles to the plane of the window. Call these cards i and ii
respectively. Now look at the cards from a position in the room
such that the horizon is plainly visible through the window and
your C.V.R. is at right angles to the plane of the window.

How is your picture plane situated?

Change your eye-line and mark its new position on the wall.

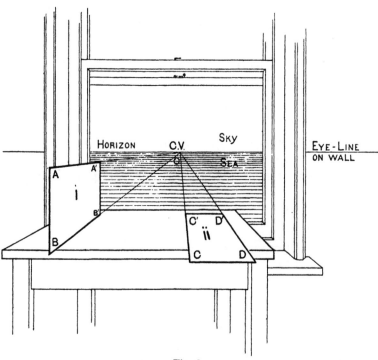

Fig. 3

1. Let AB be the nearer vertical edge of the card i. It will
be noticed that AA' and BB' appear to meet on the horizon or
eye-line, which may be marked on the window pane.

If this card were to be indefinitely prolonged through the
window, the projection of its further edge on the picture plane
would ultimately vanish.

Since *AA'* and *BB'* are *horizontal and parallel* straight lines they are parallel to the horizontal plane through your eye and therefore meet it at an infinite distance. This is shown by the fact that they appear to meet on the horizon, which we assume to be in the horizontal plane through your eye, though strictly speaking the visible horizon is always below this plane. The dip of the horizon is, however, a small angle and for the purposes of drawing we are justified in making the above assumption.

2. Let *CD* be the nearer horizontal edge of the card ii. It will be noticed here that *CC'* and *DD'* appear to meet on the eye-line, for they are *horizontal and parallel*. Let *O* be the point in which they meet the eye-line.

Do *AA'* and *BB'* appear to pass through *O*? If so, why?

Can you mention any other straight lines in the figure that appear to pass through *O*?

Do all straight lines parallel to *CC'* appear to pass through *O*?

Do all horizontal lines appear to pass through *O*?

The straight lines *AA'*, *BB'*, *CC'* and *DD'* are said to *vanish* at the point *O*, which is called the *vanishing point* of these lines, and since they are at right angles to the P.P. this point is the C.V.

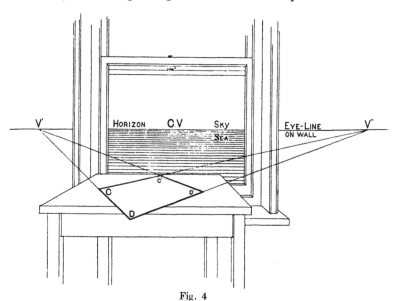

Fig. 4

If the card ii be now turned round on the table (fig. 4), CD and $C'D'$ are no longer parallel to the eye-line and CC' and DD' are no longer at right angles to the P.P. so do not vanish at the C.V.

We can imagine the rectangle to be prolonged indefinitely either in the direction of CC' or in the direction of DC, and in both cases the projection on the P.P. of the remote side of the rectangle will ultimately vanish. In this position of the card, therefore, the sides of the rectangle vanish at points V' and V'', situated on the horizon, one on either side of the C.V. The position of the invisible part of the horizon may be marked on the wall.

If the card is gradually turned round into its former position V'' approaches and V' moves further away from the C.V., and finally when CC' is again at right angles to the P.P. V'' is at the C.V. and CD and $C'D'$ are *parallel to the eye-line*, along which V' has moved to an infinite distance.

The perspective centre of a straight line.

In fig. 5 a part of the eye-line is seen with the vanishing point of the two horizontal and parallel straight lines which respectively join the tops and bottoms of a straight row of equal posts, placed at equal distances apart on the same horizontal level.

The positions of the posts AF and CH are given. BG is then determined by drawing the diagonals of the rectangle $ACHF$, which intersect in X. A central horizontal line XYZ can then be drawn, meeting the post CH in the point Y.

$ACHF$ is a rectangle whose diagonals bisect one another geometrically and therefore perspectively, that is, AH and FC bisect each other at X. Moreover AC and FH are bisected at B and G. In general a straight line may be perspectively bisected by completing any parallelogram of which it is a diagonal, and inserting the other diagonal. (See fig. 12 (a).)

On joining GY and producing it to meet the upper line in D we obtain the position of the fourth post DK, whose middle point is Z.

Similarly by joining HZ and producing it to meet the upper line in E we obtain the position of the fifth post EN, and so on.

The obliques FC, GD, HE, etc., are the diagonals of equal

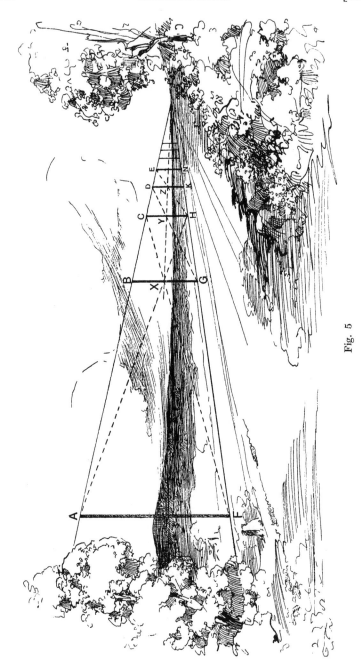

Fig. 5

rectangles and being parallel vanish at an *incidental point* vertically above the vanishing point of the horizontal lines.

Where is the vanishing point of the obliques *AH*, *BK*, *CN*, etc.?

After a short experience the correct perspective centre of a straight line may be judged with comparative accuracy.

Practise bisecting lines in perspective and confirming by geometry.

When the eye-line is within the limits of the paper on which we make our drawing, the division of a horizontal straight line into *n* equal parts in perspective may be performed as follows.

Let *ab* be the given horizontal straight line in perspective, and let it meet the eye-line in the point *O*. Through either extremity

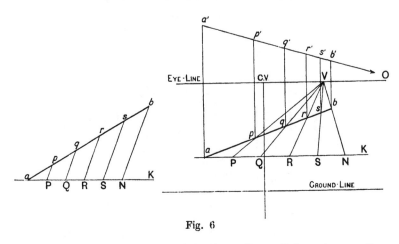

Fig. 6

of the line, e.g. *a*, draw a straight line *aK* parallel to the eye-line, and along *aK* mark off *n* convenient equal lengths *aP*, *PQ*, ... *SN*. Join *Nb* and produce to meet the eye-line in the point *V*. Join *VP*, *VQ*, ... *VS* cutting *ab* in the points *p*, *q*, ... *s*.

Then *p*, *q*, ... *s* divide *ab* into *n* perspectively equal parts.

For since *Pp*, *Qq*, ... *Nb* vanish at a point *V* they are parallel, and since they divide the straight line *aN* into *n* equal parts, they divide into *n* equal parts any other straight line drawn from *a* and terminated by *VN*.

If straight lines *aa'*, *pp'*, ... *bb'* are drawn at right angles to the eye-line to meet any straight line through *O* in the points

a', p', ... b' then aa', pp', ... bb' are equal vertical lines and $app'a'$, $pqq'p'$, ... $sbb's'$ are equal rectangles in a vertical plane.

How could you by this method divide into n equal parts an oblique straight line, of which the orthogonal projection on the ground plane is given?

Having given in fig. 5 the height of the first post AF and the distance between the first two posts FG construct by this method the next four posts.

Use this construction (i) to bisect, (ii) to trisect a horizontal straight line in perspective and (iii) to produce such a straight line a distance equal to its own length. These three constructions may be found to be of use.

Suppose we have a number of equal rectangles $ABCD, A'B'C'D'$, $A''B''C''D''$, ... placed in parallel vertical planes with their equal sides DC, $D'C'$, $D''C''$, ... in the same horizontal plane (fig. 7).

Are AB, $A'B'$, $A''B''$, ... also in a horizontal plane?

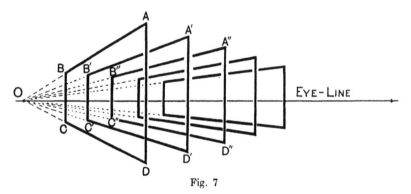

Fig. 7

Suppose also that D, D', D'', ... are in the same straight line.

Are A, A', A'', ... in the same straight line and is this line horizontal? Are B, B', B'', ... in a straight line? and are C, C', C'', ...?

DC, $D'C'$, $D''C''$, ... being *horizontal and parallel* straight lines vanish at some point O in the eye-line, and AB, $A'B'$, $A''B''$, ... also vanish at some point in the eye-line.

Is this point the same as O? Why? What rectangular planes in a room can you give as illustrations?

Now consider equal rectangles $ABCD$, $A'B'C'D'$, $A''B''C''D''$, ... placed in parallel horizontal planes so that A, A', A'', ... are in the same vertical line and AB, $A'B'$, $A''B''$ are parallel (fig. 8).

Then *AD* and *BC* are *horizontal and parallel* straight lines and vanish at some point *O* in the eye-line. *A'D'* and *B'C'* also vanish at some point in the eye-line.

Is this point the same as *O*? Why?
Do all the straight lines *A"D"*, *A'''D'''*, ... and *B"C"*, *B'''C'''*, ... vanish at *O*?

For a similar reason *BA* and *CD* vanish at some point *P* in the eye-line, and, moreover, *B'A'*, *B"A"*, ... and *C'D'*, *C"D"*, ... all vanish at *P*.

What planes in a room or building can you give as illustrations?

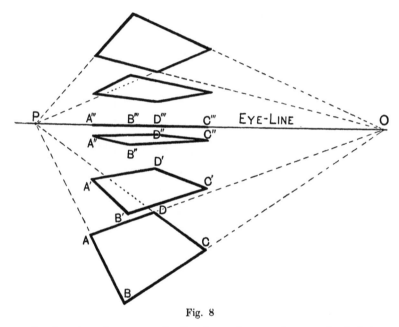

Fig. 8

In drawing the rectangle the importance of correctly judging the apparent size of the nearest right angle cannot be unduly emphasized.

In fig. 7 the points *D*, *D'*, *D"*, ... are all in the same horizontal line, but at different distances from the picture plane. Notice carefully that in this figure the angles *ADC*, *A'D'C'*, ..., lying in parallel vertical planes, become more nearly a right angle as *D* recedes from the picture plane.

In fig. 8 the points *B*, *B'*, *B"*, ... are at the same distance from the picture plane, lying in horizontal planes, but at different levels. Here the right angles ABC, $A'B'C'$, ... become more altered as they approach the eye-level, where the angle appears as a straight angle.

Place on a table near a window a rectangular card, $EE'F'F$, with its plane inclined to the horizontal and with EE' horizontal and inclined to the plane of the window (fig. 9). Let EF be the nearer oblique edge. Then EE' and FF' vanish at a point O in the eye-line.

Do FE and $F'E'$ appear to meet?
Do they meet at a point in the eye-line?

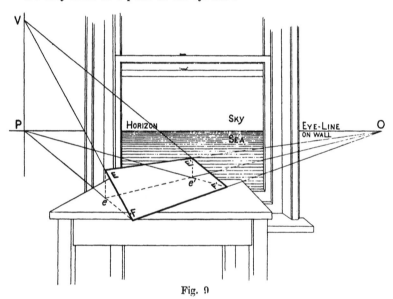

Fig. 9

Let e and e' be the orthogonal projections on the plane of the table of the points E and E'. Then Fe and $F'e'$ vanish at some point P in the eye-line.

Draw PV at right angles to the eye-line and parallel to the P.P. to meet FE produced in V. Then PV is the apparent line of intersection of the two parallel vertical planes EeF and $E'e'F'$.

EF and $E'F'$ are two lines in these planes and their vanishing point must lie in both planes and therefore is a point in PV. So FE and $F'E'$ vanish at V, which is called an *incidental vanishing point*.

We see that we can find the vanishing point of a pair of oblique parallel straight lines by finding first the vanishing point of their orthogonal projections on the ground plane.

Do all oblique straight lines parallel to EF or $E'F'$ vanish at V?

Do all oblique straight lines vanish at V?

If FF' is kept fixed but the card is rotated about it so that the acute angle it makes with the horizontal plane continually increases, the vanishing point of FE and $F'E'$ moves along PV away from P.

If EFe be made a right angle where is this vanishing point?

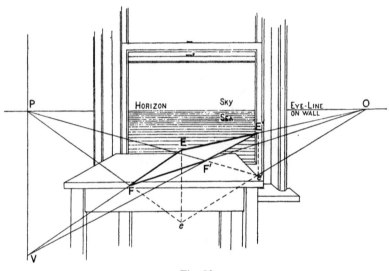

Fig. 10

In the latter case the plane of the card is vertical and EF and $E'F'$ are vertical.

Where is the vanishing point of all vertical lines?

Are vertical lines always represented at right angles to and horizontal lines parallel to the eye-line on the P.P.?

If the card is rotated until it is in the position shown in fig.10, the vanishing point V of EF and $E'F'$ will be seen to be *below* the eye-line, but to lie on the same straight line at right angles to the eye-line as before, since the point P, at which eF and $e'F'$ now vanish, is the same.

Take a piece of cardboard $ABB'A'C'C$ of the shape shown in fig. 11. $BB'C'C$ is a rectangle and ABC and $A'B'C'$ are equal isosceles triangles.

Cut along BC and $B'C'$ halfway through the thickness of the card and bend the triangles ABC and $A'B'C'$ into parallel planes.

Hold the card so that A and A' appear on your eye-line and BC or $B'C'$ is vertical. Suppose that AB and $A'B'$ appear to

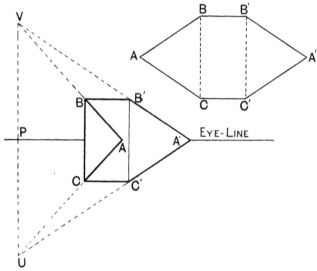

Fig. 11

meet at V and that AC and $A'C'$ appear to meet at U. If the straight line joining VU appears to cross the eye-line at P, we have from the symmetry of the figure that VU is at right angles to the eye-line and PV is equal to PU.

We have seen that all straight lines parallel to AB or $A'B'$ vanish at V and that all straight lines parallel to AC or $A'C'$ vanish at U. These straight lines lie in parallel vertical planes and are equally inclined to the ground plane.

Straight lines, therefore, that are in parallel vertical planes, and are equally inclined to the ground plane vanish in one or other of two points, which lie on a straight line at right angles to the eye-line and are equidistant from the eye-line.

Consider a number of equal rectangles $A'B'C'D'$, $A''B''C'D'$, $A''B''C''D''$, ... placed as in fig. 12 (a) to form a series of roofs, the troughs $A'B'$, $A''B''$, ... being in the same horizontal plane. Then the edges $A'D'$, $A''D'$, $A''D''$, ... are in a vertical plane as also are $B'C'$, $B''C'$, $B''C''$, ...

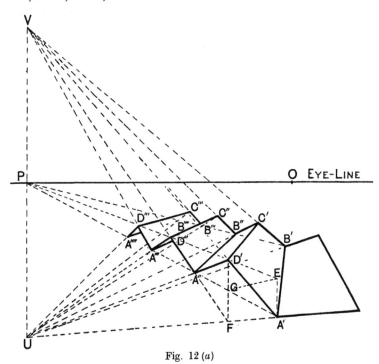

Fig. 12 (a)

$A'A''A'''$ ..., $B'B''B'''$ ..., $C'C''C'''$ ... and $D'D''D''$ ... are *horizontal and parallel* straight lines and vanish at some point P in the eye-line. $A'B'$, $D'C'$, $A''B''$, $D''C''$, ... for the same reason vanish at some point O in the eye-line.

$A'D'$, $A''D''$, ... and $B'C'$, $B''C''$, ... being parallel obliques vanish at some point V above and $D'A''$, $D''A'''$, ... and $C'B''$, $C''B'''$, ... similarly vanish at some point U below the eye-line.

What do you know concerning PU and PV?
What are the angles VPO and UPO?
Do all obliques parallel to $A'D'$ vanish at V?
Do all obliques parallel to $A''D'$ vanish at U?

If the pitch of one of the roofs is altered the vanishing points of its oblique edges are no longer at V and U but still lie at equal distances from P in the straight line VPU.

If $D''A''$ meets $A'U$ in F, the figure $A'D'A''F$ is the perspective projection of a rhombus in a vertical plane. The diagonals $A'A''$ and $D'F$, therefore, are the projections of straight lines which bisect one another at right angles, and, since $A'A''$ represents a horizontal line, $D'F$ represents a vertical line and is therefore parallel to VU.

If $A'A''$ and $D'F$ intersect in G, G is the perspective centre of the straight line $A'A''$ (see p. 135).

Why are the projections $D'G$ and GF equal in length?

To find the vertical bisector in perspective of a horizontal straight line $A'A''$, when the eye-line is given, we may make use of the following construction.

Through P, the point in which $A'A''$ meets the eye-line, draw VPU at right angles to the eye-line and mark off PV equal to PU.

Then through V and U draw the pairs of lines passing through A' and A'' to form the figure $A'D'A''F$.

$D'F$ cuts $A'A''$ in the perspective centre of $A'A''$ and is the vertical bisector. In roof structure this would give the position of the king-post.

To find the perspective centre of an oblique $A'D'$ we may proceed as follows.

Through P, the point in which the eye-line is cut by the straight line $A'G$, the orthogonal projection of $A'D'$ on a horizontal plane through A', draw PD' and through A' draw $A'E$ at right angles to the eye-line to meet PD' in E.

Then $EA'GD'$ is the perspective projection of a rectangle and EG cuts $A'D'$ in its perspective centre.

In fig. 12 (b) the roofs have been separated but the walls of the buildings supporting them are still parallel, so the sets of edges in plan vanish at P and O and the oblique edges at V and U.

Are the roofs equally inclined to the H.P.?

Ex. Draw a similar diagram in which the roofs are inclined at different angles to the H.P.

Where are the four incidental vanishing points in this case?

We have considered some of the geometrical properties of the rectangle and the manner in which its sides vanish in perspective.

Let us now consider the apparent size of the rectangle as it is rotated.

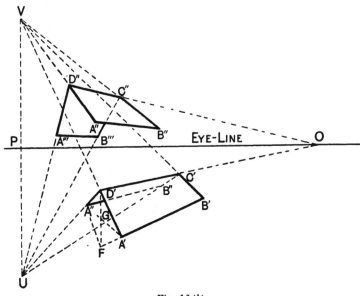

Fig. 12 (b)

Hold a rectangular card at the eye-level, with a short edge horizontal and parallel to the P.P. Rotate it about the nearer short edge. As the further edge rises or falls the apparent size of the rectangle increases.

Continue the rotation and note what you observe.
In what manner do the right angles appear to change?

We have a practical example in the following.

As a buttress rises, the lateral pressure to which it is subjected diminishes and consequently its horizontal cross-section is reduced. This is accomplished in stages and weatherings are introduced.

In fig. 13 rectangular weatherings are considered. If the angles of slope at all stages were the same, the apparent size

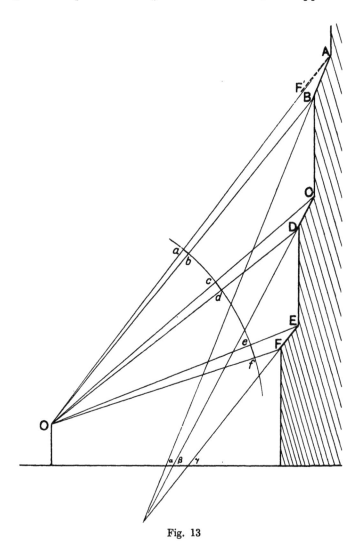

Fig. 13

of the weatherings, as seen in the position O, would diminish as the view is directed upwards, and probably an unsuitable proportion would arise. In order to arrange better the apparent sizes of the weatherings, their slopes vary, the inclination of the weathering to the ground increasing with its height above the ground.

In the figure the straight lines AB, CD, and EF are the sections of three weatherings on a buttress, made by a vertical plane at right angles to the plane of the weatherings, and make angles α, β and γ with the ground.

If O is the position in this vertical plane of the eye of a spectator and a circle is drawn to cut the straight lines OA, OB, ... in the points a, b, ... then the relative apparent sizes of the weatherings are measured by the lengths of the arcs ab, cd, and ef.

AF' is drawn parallel to EF. If all the weatherings had the inclination of the lowest the top one would be invisible to the eye at O.

Thus we find that as the plane of the rectangle varies in its slope the apparent size of the visible surface varies also.

The rotation of a door on its hinges offers another practical example. Carefully consider the variation in the apparent size of the right angles (see fig. 17).

For changes in the apparent area of the rectangle in oblique positions see fig. 25.

I. *Straight lines at right angles to the picture plane.*

In fig. 14 E represents the position of the eye of the spectator and EO is a straight line drawn at right angles to the P.P., meeting it in the point O, which is therefore the C.V. of the spectator.

AB is a straight line at right angles to the P.P. and BA produced meets the P.P. in the point R.

Then RB and EO are parallel and therefore lie in the same plane.

Hence the straight lines EA and EB meet the straight line OR in points a and b respectively, and the straight line ab is the perspective projection of AB on the picture plane. We thus see that ab passes through O, and hence obtain:

LAW I. *Straight lines which are at right angles to the picture plane vanish at the* C.V.

10—2

II. *Parallel straight lines parallel to the picture plane.*

In fig. 14 CD is a straight line parallel to the P.P. and EC and ED meet the P.P. in the points c and d respectively. Then the straight line cd is the perspective projection of CD on the picture plane.

Since CD is parallel to the P.P. it can never meet it and therefore can never meet any straight line in the P.P.

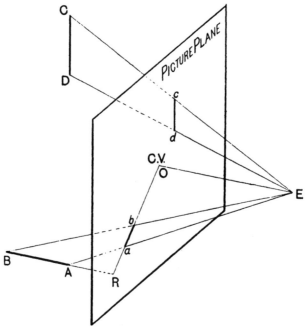

Fig. 14

Hence CD can never meet cd and lies in the same plane as cd.

Therefore cd is parallel to CD.

We thus obtain:

LAW II. *Parallel straight lines which are parallel to the picture plane have parallel projections on the picture plane, i.e. are drawn actually parallel in their perspective representations.*

COR. Those which are horizontal are parallel to the eye-line.

III. *Horizontal and parallel straight lines.*

In fig. 15 E represents the eye of the spectator, and a vertical line EF meets the ground plane in the point F. AB is a horizontal straight line meeting the P.P. in the point P.

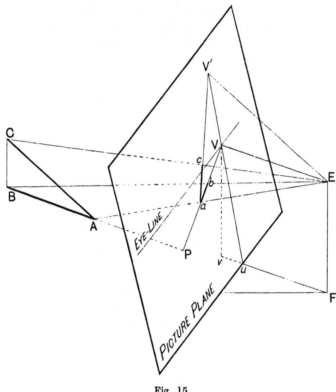

Fig. 15

EV is a straight line parallel to AB and is therefore horizontal and meets the eye-line in some point V.

Since AB and EV are parallel they lie in the same plane and therefore the straight lines EA and EB meet the straight line PV in points a and b respectively. The straight line ab is the perspective projection of AB on the picture plane.

But V is a fixed point if the direction of AB is given.

Hence we obtain:

LAW III. *Straight lines which are horizontal and parallel vanish at some point in the eye-line.*

IV. *Parallel straight lines which are oblique to the picture plane and are not horizontal.*

In fig. 15 BC is a vertical line drawn through B and AC represents an oblique. Then ABC is a vertical plane.

Through E the straight line EV' is drawn parallel to AC to meet the P.P. in the point V'. Then EVV' is a vertical plane. Fu is drawn parallel to EV to meet the ground line in the point u and therefore lies in the vertical plane EVV'.

Hence uV is the line of intersection of this plane with the P.P. and therefore V' lies in uV.

AC and EV' lie in the same plane and therefore the straight line EC meets the straight line aV' in some point c and ac is the perspective projection of AC on the picture plane.

But V' is a fixed point if the direction of AC is given.

Hence we obtain:

LAW IV. *Parallel straight lines which are inclined to the picture plane and are not horizontal vanish at some point not in the eye-line.*

The following is a general statement of the above laws:

All horizontal and parallel straight lines vanish at a point in the eye-line (horizon). If they are parallel to the P.P. *the vanishing point lies at infinity, and if at right angles to the* P.P. *the* C.V. *is the vanishing point. All other parallel straight lines which are not horizontal vanish at some point not in the eye-line.*

If the picture plane is vertical, VV' is also vertical, since it is now the line of intersection of two vertical planes. In this case, then, VV' is at right angles to the eye-line.

The results embodied in these four laws are true whether the picture plane is vertical or oblique.

The student should now make a careful study of figs. 1 (*a*) and 1 (*b*). Here we have a double projection. A perspective drawing is given of what an eye X might see if we constructed the lines in space necessary for the projection of the rectangle $ABCD$ on the eye E's picture plane.

In both figures the P.P. for E is supposed to be limited in size and rectangular, with one pair of edges horizontal. This pair meet on X's eye-line at the point O.

The sides of the rectangle $ABCD$ vanish in pairs at the points V' and V'' on X's eye-line and the sides of the projected figure $a'b'c'd'$ vanish at points v' and v'' on E's eye-line. If the drawing is correctly made $Ev'V'$ and $Ev''V''$ are straight lines.

In fig. 1 (a) the vertical edges of E's picture plane being parallel to X's picture plane are drawn parallel and at right angles to X's eye-line. In fig. 1 (b) the oblique edges of E's picture plane vanish at some point (U' say) not on X's eye-line. Ff is at right angles to E's picture line and is therefore parallel to the orthogonal projection of these obliques on the ground plane. If then Ff meets X's eye-line in the point U, UU' is at right angles to this eye-line.

The straight line through f and the c.v., being at right angles to the picture line, is parallel to these obliques and therefore also vanishes at the point U'.

Shadows of Rectangles in Perspective

In fig. 16 $PQRS$ is a horizontal rectangle and we suppose the plane B to be temporarily removed. Then $p'q'r's'$ is the shadow of $PQRS$ cast on a horizontal plane A which may be taken to be the ground plane. $pqrs$ is the orthogonal projection of $PQRS$ on the plane A, or on the plane produced, so Pp, Qq, Rr and Ss are vertical straight lines and are therefore at right angles to the eye-line.

$p'p$, $q'q$, $r'r$ and $s's$ are *horizontal and parallel* straight lines and therefore vanish at some point V in the eye-line (see pp. 25 and 172).

$p'P$, $q'Q$, $r'R$ and $s'S$, being drawn in the direction of the sun's rays, are parallel obliques and therefore vanish at some point O not in the eye-line but in the straight line VO which is drawn through V at right angles to the eye-line.

PQ, SR, pq, sr, $p'q'$ and $s'r'$ are *horizontal and parallel* straight lines and therefore vanish at a point V' in the eye-line

Which straight lines vanish at V'' and why do they vanish at the same point?

If the sun is in front of the spectator, as in the figure, the points p', q', r' and s' of the shadow are nearer the P.P than the corresponding points p, q, r and s of the orthogonal

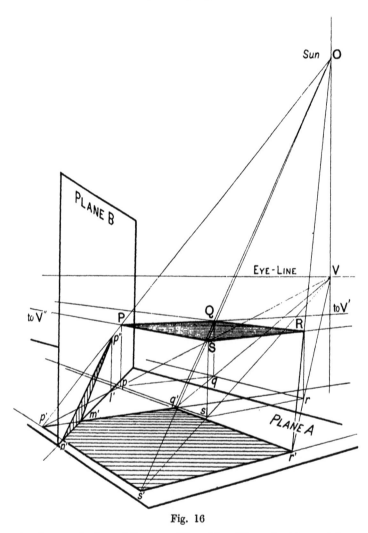

Fig. 16

projection and the obliques $p'P$, $q'Q$, $r'R$ and $s'S$ vanish at a point O *above* the eye-line.

If, however, the sun is behind the spectator (fig. 17), the

points p', q', r' and s' are further from the P.P. than the corresponding points p, q, r and s, and now the obliques Pp', Qq', Rr' and Ss' vanish at a point below the eye-line.

Introduce the plane B vertically so that its line of intersection with the plane A cuts the shadow edges $p'q'$ and $p's'$ in the points m' and n' and cuts pp' in the point l'. To construct the point p'' in which Op' meets the plane B draw $l'p''$ vertical, i.e. parallel to pP, to meet Pp' in the point p''.

Then $n'p''$ and $m'p''$ are the edges of the shadow cast on the plane B.

In fig. 17 the shadow of an open door is shown as cast upon the adjacent wall and floor. The door is represented by the rectangle $PQRS$, QR being the axis about which the door turns.

The C.V.R. of the spectator is at right angles to the wall and therefore the P.P. is parallel to the wall. Thus the line of intersection of the wall (plane B) and the floor (plane A) is parallel to the P.P. and, since it is horizontal, it is therefore drawn parallel to the eye-line. (Law II, Cor.)

The sun is behind the spectator so the sun's rays vanish at some point O *below* the eye-line.

$p'q'$ is the shadow of PQ on the ground if the plane B be supposed to be removed. Hence Rq' and Sp' are *horizontal and parallel* straight lines and vanish at some point V in the eye-line. Moreover we know that VO is at right angles to the eye-line (see p. 27).

What other set of straight lines vanish at a point in the eye-line, and why?

Let the plane B be now introduced and suppose Sp' cuts it in the point l.

Since SPp' is a vertical plane, if we draw the vertical line lp'' it will meet Pp' in a point p'' which lies in the plane of the wall.

Hence p'' is the shadow of P as thrown on the wall and the shadow edges Qp'', $p''l$ and lS of the door are thus determined.

Ex. Make a similar drawing with the door in the position indicated by $P'QRS'$, and, assuming the sun to be in the same position, construct the shadow of the door as cast upon the wall and floor. When panels are shown in the door, several lines are introduced which will vanish with the edges of the door.

It may be interesting to learn that the Greeks used methods of framing wood similar to those employed to-day.

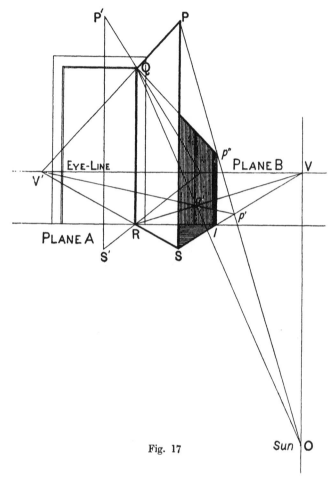

Fig. 17

RECTANGULAR FORMS

In the following examples make bold sketches. Finish your work neatly, varying the strength of line, and put in what artistic effect you can. Use tracing-paper to find the vanishing points and eye-line.

Example I.   A Wall

Fig. 18 represents the side of an ordinary wall.

Find the vanishing point of the horizontal lines and also the incidental vanishing points of the diagonals of the bricks.   What are their positions?

Draw the wall also as seen from a different position, changing the height of the eye.

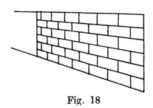

Fig. 18

Example II.   A Floor

Fig. 19 represents a simple tiled floor.

Find the vanishing points of the edges and the eye-line.   Find also the vanishing points of the diagonals of the tiles.   Test whether C is the perspective centre of AB.

Draw the floor also as seen from a different position, changing the height of the eye as before.

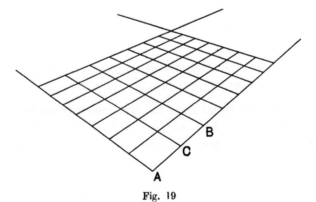

Fig. 19

Example III.   A Roof

Fig. 20 represents part of a tiled roof.

Find the vanishing point of the horizontal edges and the eye-line.   Find also the incidental vanishing point of the oblique edges of the tiles.
Do the diagonals of the tiles also vanish?   If so, where?

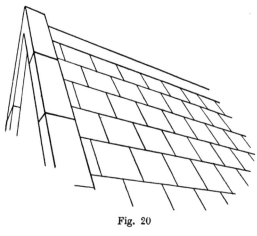

Fig. 20

Ex.   Sketch a portion of fig. 27, Herring-Bone (Part I) in perspective.   Let the vertical plane in which it lies vanish to the left at an angle of about 60° with the P.P.

Ex.   Suppose fig. 40 (Part I) to lie in an H.P., slightly to the right and above the eye-line with the long edges of the bottom link parallel to the P.P.   Sketch it in perspective.

REFLECTIONS OF RECTANGLES AT PLANE SURFACES AS VIEWED WITH THE C.V.R. HORIZONTAL

A point has its image along the perpendicular drawn through it to the reflecting surface and the point and its image are equidistant from the surface.   This leads at once to the following statements:

(i)   A straight line and its image are collinear when the straight line is at right angles to the reflecting surface.

(ii)   A straight line and its image are parallel when the straight line is parallel to the reflecting surface.

In (i) we have a sure test of the perpendicularity of a straight line to a surface.

In general for any straight line the perpendiculars drawn to the surface from the extremities of the line are those which chiefly concern us in the construction of the perspective representation of its image.

In figs. R 1 and R 2 the reflection of a rectangle $ABCD$ is seen in a plane surface which is at right angles to the P.P. The side AB is parallel to the surface. In fig. R 1 the plane of the rectangle is at right angles to and in fig. R 2 inclined obliquely to the reflecting surface.

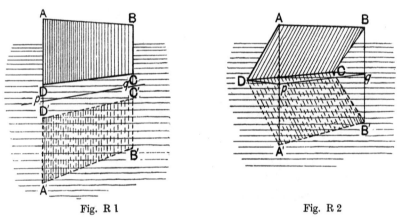

Fig. R 1   Fig. R 2

A' and B' are the images of A and B respectively. The straight lines AA' and BB' are at right angles to the surface and therefore parallel to the picture plane, and if they intersect the surface in the points p and q respectively Ap and pA' are of equal length as also are Bq and qB'.

In fig. R 3 the reflection of a rectangle $ABCD$ is seen in a plane surface which is inclined obliquely to the P.P. In this case the straight lines AA' and BB' are not parallel to the P.P., but vanish at an incidental point and therefore p and q, the points in which AA' and BB' meet the plane surface, are their perspective centres.

It is important to observe that the orthogonal projections of AD and BC on the reflecting surface are parallel. In fig. R 2 they are horizontal and therefore vanish at a point in the eye-line, but in fig. R 3 they are generally not horizontal and therefore vanish at an incidental point.

In each case, since AB is parallel to the surface, the image $A'B'$ is parallel to AB and therefore vanishes with it at some point. In figs. R 1 and R 2 this point is in the eye-line, but in fig. R 3 it is an incidental point.

How would you arrange the rectangle $ABCD$ in fig. R 3 so that the orthogonal projection of AD on the surface is horizontal?

Ex. Cut out a stiff rectangular piece of paper, and lean it against a window pane. Sketch it and its reflection.

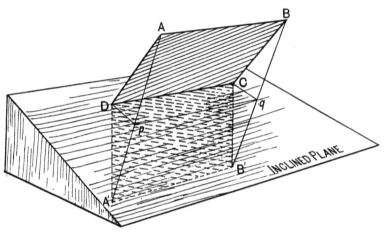

Fig. R 3

RECTANGULAR PRISMS

Two rectangular prisms are shown in perspective in fig. 21. One of them, $PQRSpqrs$, rests on the H.P. with its edges PS, ps, QR and qr at right angles to the P.P. and consequently with its edges PQ, pq, SR and sr parallel to the P.P. The other prism, $ABCDabcd$, rests on the face $PQRS$ with its edges Aa, Bb, Cc and Dd vertical, but with its vertical faces inclined to the P.P.

PS, ps, QR and qr being *at right angles to the* P.P. vanish at the C.V. (Law I).

PQ, pq, SR and *sr* being *parallel to the* P.P. have parallel projections on the P.P. (Law II). Since they are horizontal they are drawn parallel to the eye-line (Cor.).

Similarly, *Aa, Bb, ..., Pp, Qq, ...*, being parallel to the P.P. have parallel projections on the P.P. Since they are vertical they are drawn at right angles to the eye-line.

AD, ad, BC and *bc* are *horizontal and parallel* straight lines, but, as they are not perpendicular to the P.P., they vanish at some point *O* in the eye-line other than the C.V. (Law III).

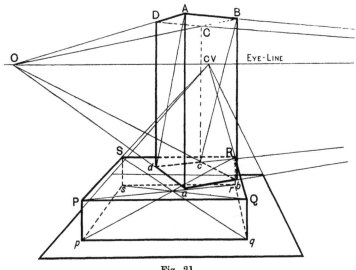

Fig. 21

For the same reason *AB, ab, DC* and *dc* vanish at some other point *V* in the eye-line, *O* and *V* being on opposite sides of the C.V.

Ad and *Bc* being parallel straight lines which are inclined to the P.P. and are not horizontal vanish at some point not in the eye-line (Law IV). Observe that the plane *ABcd* slopes downwards away from the spectator, so that *AB* is nearer than *cd* to the P.P. The projection of *AB* is thus greater than that of *cd*. This shows that the obliques *Ad* and *Bc* meet at a point below the eye-line.

The diagonals of a rectangular prism meet in a point. This is shown in the case of the lower prism, and furnishes us with a test for the correctness of our drawing.

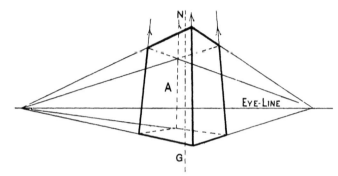

Fig. 23 (a)

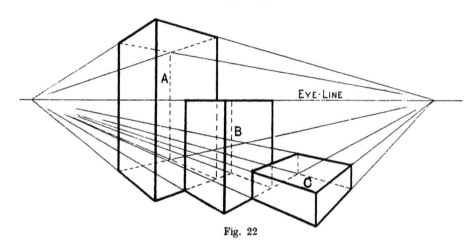

Fig. 22

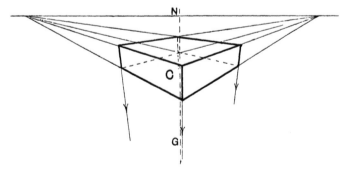

Fig. 23 (b)

A, *B* and *C* (fig. 22) represent in perspective rectangular blocks of buildings with the eye-line on the level of the roof of block *B*.

The blocks are observed as a group and it is therefore convenient to select a horizontal c.v.r., giving a vertical picture plane.

In figs. 23 (*a*) and (*b*) two of the blocks are observed separately with the c.v.r. directed approximately to the middle point of the central line *NG* of the building, giving an oblique picture plane.

The vertical sides of the blocks are no longer parallel to the p.p. and therefore vanish at some point either above or below the eye-line as shown in the figure (Law IV).

Similar results are obtained in photography, when the plate (or p.p.) is not in a vertical plane.

Perspective Views of a Rectangular Prism

In order to familiarize the student with the perspective representations of a rectangular prism as seen in different positions, series of views are given in figs. 24 and 25, which are obtained by rotating a prism about a vertical and a horizontal edge respectively.

In fig. 24 *AB* is the perspective projection of the vertical edge about which the prism is rotated. Five positions of the prism are considered and their perspective projections are numbered i, ii, iii, iv and v.

The c.v.r. is directed to a point in *BA* produced.

In position i the edges *AD* and *BC* are parallel to the p.p., so the angle *DAB* is a right angle.

Where do the edges at right angles to the face *ABCD* vanish?

As the prism is rotated about *AB* from the position i to the position iv, *AD* and the edges parallel to it become shorter whilst the edges at right angles to the face *ABCD* lengthen in their perspective representations. Also the perspective length of the edge *CD* decreases as *CD* recedes from the p.p.

In the position iv *AD* and *CD* have their shortest lengths, whilst in position v the face opposite to *ABCD* is seen.

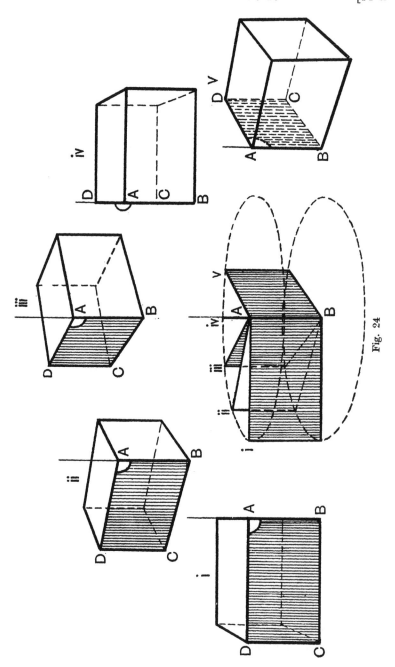

Fig. 24

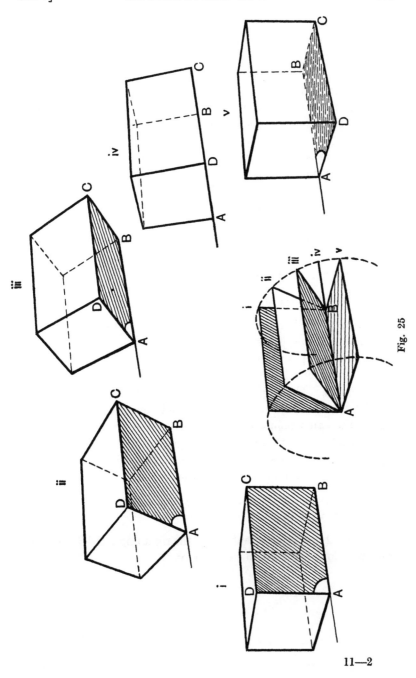

Fig. 25

11—2

The apparent lengths of AD are really controlled by the apparent lengths of the radii of a horizontal circle of which A is the centre (see fig. 82).

Carefully notice how the apparent size of the right angle BAD increases from a right angle in position i to two right angles in position iv. Compare the apparent size of the angle BAD with those of the other two angles at A in each position.

In fig. 25 AB is the perspective projection of the horizontal edge about which the prism is rotated. Five positions of the face $ABCD$ are considered and their perspective projections are numbered i, ii, iii, iv and v.

The c.v.r. is again directed to a point in the vertical line through A, and AB is inclined to the p.p.

In position i the edges AD and BC are vertical, but the angle DAB does not appear a right angle.

Where do the edges at right angles to the face $ABCD$ vanish?

As the prism is rotated about AB, from position i to position iii, the edge AD appears to decrease and pass through its shortest length between positions iii and iv. Its apparent length is that of the apparent length of the radius of a vertical circle of which A is the centre. The edge DC during its complete rotation remains parallel to the horizontal edge AB, and therefore always meets AB at the same point in the eye-line.

In positions ii, iii and iv, the edges parallel to AD and the edges at right angles to the face $ABCD$ vanish at incidental points, one above and one below the eye-line.

What is the locus of these incidental vanishing points?
Where are these points in positions i and v?

Observe how the apparent size of the right angle DAB decreases from position i to zero in position iv.

Shadows of Rectangular Prisms

In the figure *PQRSpqrs* is a rectangular prism resting with the face *pqrs* in contact with a horizontal plane *A*, which may be taken to be the ground plane.

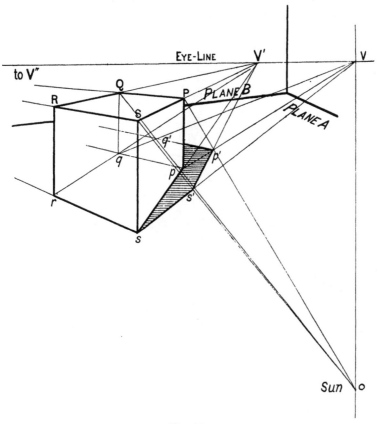

Fig. 26

The edges of the prism *RQ*, *rq*, *SP* and *sp*, being *horizontal and parallel* straight lines, vanish at a point *V'* in the eye-line and for the same reason *PQ*, *pq*, *SR* and *sr* vanish at a point *V"* in the eye-line.

The direction of the sun's rays is represented by the straight lines *Pp'*, *Qq'* and *Ss'*, *p'*, *q'* and *s'* being points in the plane *A*.

These straight lines are parallel obliques and therefore vanish at some point O, not in the eye-line. OV is drawn at right angles to the eye-line, meeting it in the point V.

pp', qq' and ss' are the orthogonal projections of Pp', Qq' and Ss' on the ground plane and therefore vanish at V.

The shadow edges $p'q'$ and $p's'$ are parallel respectively to PQ and PS and pass respectively through V'' and V'.

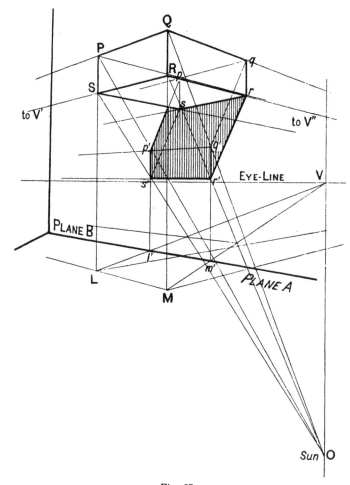

Fig. 27

The shadow consists of the two parallelograms $pqq'p'$ and $pp's's$, and is the same as that cast by the two adjacent faces $PQqp$ and $PSsp$, both of which are at right angles to the plane A (see pp. 41 and 171).

Ex. Make a similar drawing of a rectangular prism and its shadow on the ground plane when the sun's rays are more oblique. Introduce a plane B at right angles to the plane A so that the line of intersection cuts the edges $p'q'$ and $p's'$ of the shadow. Construct p'', the point in which Pp' meets the plane B, and complete the shadow as cast on the two planes.

In fig. 27 $PQRSpqrs$ is a rectangular prism resting with the face $pqrs$ in contact with a vertical plane B. The line of intersection, $l'm'$, of the plane B and the ground plane A is shown.

The edges of the prism QP, qp, RS, rs being *horizontal and parallel* straight lines vanish at a point V' in the eye-line, and for the same reason the edges Pp, Qq, Rr and Ss vanish at a point V'' in the eye-line.

The direction of the sun's rays is represented by the straight lines Pp', Qq', Rr' and Ss', p', q', r' and s' being points in the plane B. These straight lines are parallel obliques and therefore vanish at some point O, not in the eye-line. OV is drawn at right angles to the eye-line meeting it in the point V.

Ll' and Mm' are the orthogonal projections of Ss' and Rr' on the ground plane and therefore vanish at V (see p. 42).

Ex. Give a drawing of a flight of steps (p. 45) the long edges of which vanish at a point to the left of the c.v. Show shadows and add some interesting surroundings.

SKETCHING

Lay tracing-paper over the following illustrations, produce the vanishing lines and thereby determine the position of the eye-line.

Example I. A Timbered Ceiling

In the figure the back wall is parallel to the picture plane of
the spectator and the lines of the main beams are all at right
angles to this plane and therefore, by Law I, these lines
vanish at a point (c.v.) in the eye-line immediately opposite
the eye.

The lines of the smaller beams are at right angles to those of
the main beams, i.e. are parallel to the picture plane. By Law II

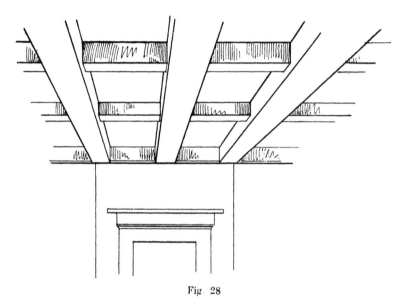

Fig. 28

they are therefore parallel in the drawing and as they are horizontal they are drawn parallel to the eye-line.

After you have studied the figure, draw it from memory, introducing what
artistic effect you can.

In this illustration we have the interpenetration of rectangular
prisms. The structure is shown in its simplest form. If the
beams are of equal cross-section and the interspaces panelled,
the ceiling is coffered.

Example II.　A Bracket

In the figure an oblique picture plane has been used with the C.V.R. directed upwards towards the middle point of the top face of the bracket, which is being viewed above our eye-line as a single object and not as part of a whole. A camera directed along the same C.V.R. would produce a picture with similar effects, if its plate were in a plane at right angles to the C.V.R.

Key　　　　　　　　Fig. 29

The bracket shows three horizontal and three vertical receding planes, and there are two sets of *horizontal and parallel* lines which vanish respectively to the right and left at points in the eye-line.

All vertical lines vanish at a point above the eye-line, situated on the straight line drawn through the middle point of the top face at right angles to the eye-line.

Give a drawing of the bracket as seen in another position with a horizontal C.V.R., the direction of the main lines being suggested in the key. Show shadows with the sun in the position indicated in the figure.

Example III. A Doorway

It is clear that in the figure there are no lines at right angles to the picture plane and therefore no lines vanishing at the c.v., but at two points in the eye-line, one on either side of the c.v.

Draw the figure from memory.

Fig. 30

Example IV. A Font

Give a drawing of the font as you would see it from another position. The key suggests the view to be drawn, where the c.v.r. is not horizontal but directed downwards to the near corner of the font. Omit the drawing of the circle, but insert the ornament if you have time. Introduce a light and shade effect with the sun in front (see p. 165).

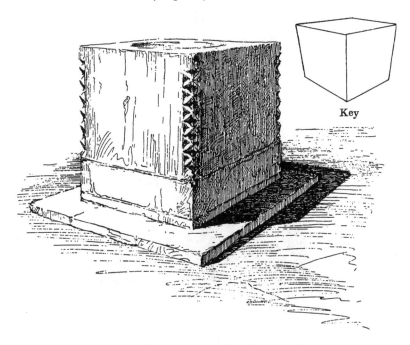

Key

Fig. 31. The font at Twyford, Leicestershire

This basin for holding the water used in the rite of baptism is generally of stone.

It superseded the ancient baptistery and was employed for the immersion of infants until the time of the Reformation. In mediaeval churches it was usually hollowed out from a solid block of stone and its form varied. It generally stands at the west end of the church.

Example V.　A suggested origin of the Corinthian Capital

Give a memory sketch of the arrangement shown (see p. 152).

The story underlying this suggestion is interesting. After the burial of a maid of Corinth the things which had delighted her on earth were put into a basket, carried to the grave and

Fig. 32

covered with a tile. By chance this basket was placed over an acanthus root. When the leaves of the plant appeared in the spring-time, they assumed, under the constraint of the basket and the corners of the tile, the form of volutes. Callimachus, a Greek architect, noticed the artistic effect, which suggested to him a new design for the capitals of his columns.

Example VI. A Rock-cut Tomb

Give a view of the tomb as seen by the eye looking down from the left with the c.v.r. horizontal, the position being suggested by the key. Shade your drawing, with the sun on your right.

In Asia Minor rock-cut tombs have been discovered which are attributed to about the seventh century B.C. and show the first work in stone of a nation of shipbuilders.

At Myra, in Lycia, we notice the imitation in stone of the timber work of a vessel. In later tombs the resemblance to shipwrights' work disappears.

Key

Fig. 33. A Rock-cut Tomb at Myra, in Lycia

Example VII. A Spiral Stairway

The figure shows a few steps of a spiral stairway. The risers A, B, C, ... are in vertical planes, one of which, A, is parallel to the P.P., and another of which, F, is at right angles to it. Each plane has two *horizontal and parallel* edges, which vanish at points in the eye-line, and each contains the straight line $abc...$, which is the axis of the spiral. The risers being of equal height, ab, bc, cd, ... are all equal to the height of A. The vanishing points of the planes B, C, D, E approach in succession the C.V., through which the edges of F pass.

Give a sketch of the stairway with the spiral reversed, showing three steps between A and F instead of four as in the figure.

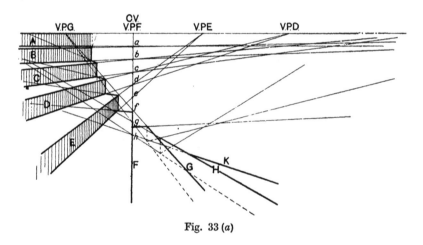

Fig. 33 (a)

CHAPTER VI

THE SQUARE AND OCTAGON

The instructions given in the preceding chapter for the treatment of the rectangle in perspective necessarily apply also to the square. A difficulty arises here, however, from the fact that the sides of the square are of equal length and the approximate estimation of their relative lengths in their perspective representations is essential and is only to be acquired after practice in drawing the square in different positions.

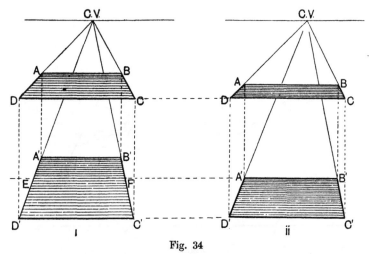

Fig. 34

In fig. 34 (i) perspective drawings of two equal rectangles $ABCD$ and $A'B'C'D'$ are shown, their corresponding sides lying in planes which are parallel to and at right angles to the P.P., whilst in (ii) two similar drawings are shown of a rectangle in which the sides AB and DC are the same length as in (i), but AD and BC are shorter.

Notice that both the angles *ADC* and *BCD* are acute.

Where does this place the position of the eye?
Which drawing is more likely to represent the perspective drawing of a square?

Cut out a square piece of cardboard and place it in various positions in front of you on the top of a table. Make sketches of the card as it appears to you, carefully judging the apparent lengths of the sides.

Are the sketches you make perspective representations of the card on a vertical picture plane or on an oblique picture plane?

The projection of a line on the picture plane is generally greater and never less than its apparent length (see Chap. v, fig. 2), the difference being small if the projection is near the c.v. In sketching the square, however, it is best to estimate the apparent lengths of the lines in the figure and make the lines of your drawing obey the laws of perspective.

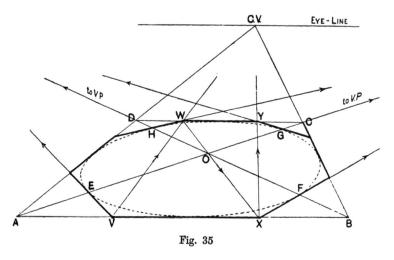

Fig. 35

In fig. 35 we have the perspective representation of an octagon inscribed in a horizontal square *ABCD*.

The sides *AB* and *DC* of the square are parallel to the P.P. and are therefore drawn parallel to the eye-line, whilst the sides *AD* and *BC*, being at right angles to the P.P., vanish at the c.v.

The diagonals AC and BD of the square intersect in the point O. The dotted curve shown is the perspective representation of the circle inscribed in the square (see Chap. VIII). Four sides of the octagon touch this circle at the points in which it meets the diagonals of the square, viz. at E, F, G and H. These sides are parallel, two and two, to the diagonals of the square and therefore vanish with them at points in the eye-line. Hence to construct the perspective representation of the octagon proceed as follows: Produce the diagonals of the square to meet the eye-line and from each of these two points draw two straight lines to touch the inscribed circle. These lines will pass through the four points E, F, G and H.

To test the correctness of your drawing the straight lines VW and XY should vanish at the c.v., whilst the four diagonals of the octagon should pass through O.

By adopting this construction you will obtain the drawing of an eight-sided figure the opposite sides of which are equal and parallel and which will be a very fair representation of a regular octagon, although your figure $ABCD$ may not be the true representation of a square.

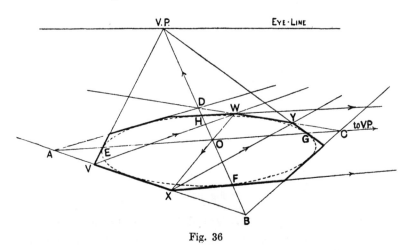

Fig. 36

In fig. 36 the plane of the square $ABCD$ is horizontal, but AD and BC are no longer at right angles to the P.P. In this case they vanish at some point in the eye-line other than the c.v., as also do *BA* and *CD*, the vanishing points being on opposite sides of the c.v.

The octagon is constructed as in fig. 35 by using the vanishing points of the diagonals of the square. Similar tests should be employed. Here *VW* and *XY* should vanish with *AD* and *BC*, and the four diagonals of the octagon should pass through the point of intersection of the diagonals of the square.

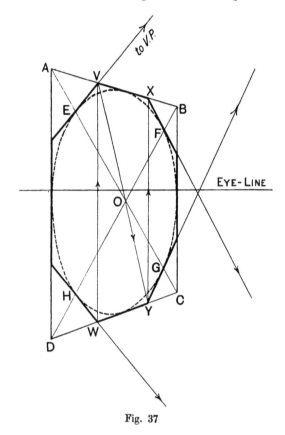

Fig. 37

Consider now a square *ABCD* and its inscribed octagon (fig. 37), placed in a vertical plane with *AB* horizontal but inclined to the P.P. *AB* and *DC* vanish at some point in the eye-line, whilst *AD* and *BC*, being vertical, are parallel to the P.P. and are drawn at right angles to the eye-line.

Where do lines parallel to the diagonals of the square vanish?

The octagon is constructed by drawing two straight lines from each of these incidental vanishing points to touch the inscribed circle.

What other straight lines not drawn in the figure vanish at these incidental points?

Test the correctness of your drawing from the fact that VW and XY are vertical and that the diagonals of the octagon and square are concurrent.

SHADOWS OF THE SQUARE AND OCTAGON IN PERSPECTIVE

In fig. 38 $PQRS$ is a horizontal square and $ABCDEFGH$ is its inscribed octagon. We suppose the plane B to be temporarily removed (see p. 53).

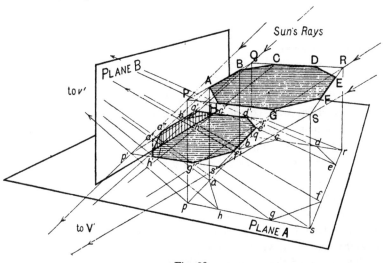

Fig. 38

$p'q'r's'$ is the shadow of $PQRS$ cast on a horizontal plane A, which may be taken to be the ground plane, and $a'b'c'd'e'f'g'h'$ is the shadow of the octagon. $pqrs$ and $abcdefgh$ are the corresponding orthogonal projections on the plane A.

12—2

Hence Pp, Aa, etc. are vertical straight lines and are therefore at right angles to the eye-line.

Ppp', Aaa', etc. are parallel vertical planes and therefore their traces pp', aa', etc. on the ground plane are *horizontal and parallel* straight lines and vanish at some point (v') in the eye-line.

Pp', Aa', etc. being in the direction of the sun's rays are parallel obliques and therefore vanish at some point (V') not in the eye-line, and $V'v'$ is at right angles to the eye-line. The sun is behind the spectator and consequently V' is below the eye-line.

The pairs of opposite sides of the shadow, e.g. $a'b'$ and $f'e'$, are parallel to the corresponding sides, e.g. AB and FE, of the octagon and therefore vanish with them at a point in the eye-line.

Introduce the vertical plane B so that its line of intersection with the plane A passes through c', cuts the shadow edge $a'h'$, and meets aa' and bb' in the points l and n. Then la'', drawn parallel to aA, meets Aa' in the point a'', the shadow of A on the plane B. Similarly the shadow of the point B on the plane B may be obtained.

In fig. 39 the shadows of a square in a vertical plane and of its inscribed octagon are shown as cast upon the ground (plane A) and a vertical wall (plane B) (see p. 55).

The sun is in front of the spectator and therefore the sun's rays vanish at a point above the eye-line.

The opposite sides of $a'b'c'd'e'f'g'h'$, the shadow figure of the octagon on the ground, are horizontal and parallel straight lines and vanish in pairs at points in the eye-line.

Ppp', Aaa', etc. are parallel vertical planes, and their traces on the ground, viz. pp', aa', etc., are horizontal and parallel straight lines and vanish at a point in the eye-line.

The trace of the plane B on the ground passes through d' and cuts the shadow edge $a'b'$. b'' and c'', the shadows of B and C on the plane B, are constructed in the same manner as described for the point A in fig. 38.

Ex. Suppose the leaded window in fig. 41 is open at right angles to the wall, and that the traces on the ground of the vertical planes containing the sun's rays make angles of 45° with the wall. Make a drawing showing the shadow on the wall of one of the octagonal lights and of one small square.

Ex. Make a similar drawing with the window open at an angle of about 120° and with the sun as before and at a convenient elevation.

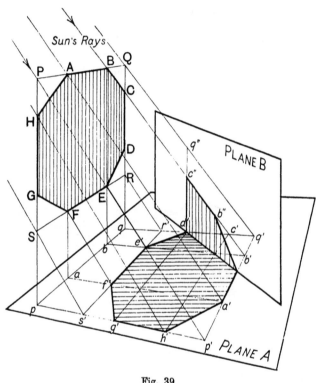

Fig. 39

Ex. Select one of the Greek frets given on p. 58 as a horizontal border on a wall about four feet from the ground. Give a sketch of a portion of it when the eye is six feet above the ground.

Ex. Show in perspective a portion of a floor tiled as in the figure on p. 52.

SQUARE AND OCTAGONAL FORMS IN PERSPECTIVE

In the two following examples make bold sketches. Finish your work neatly and put in what artistic effect you can. Use tracing-paper to find the vanishing points and eye-line.

Example I.   A Floor

Fig. 40 represents a floor with square tiles of two shades. The sides of the border squares are parallel to the sides of the room, whilst the others are placed diagonally.

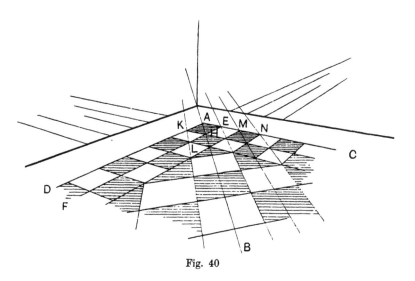

Fig. 40

Let AC and AD be the sides of the outer square in perspective. Carefully judge the direction of the diagonal BA. Mark off AE to represent the length of one side of one small square. Through E draw HE vanishing with DA and cutting AB in H, and through H draw HK vanishing with CA and cutting AD in K. Through K draw another diagonal vanishing with BA. This will give L on EF, and so on. By this means we find lengths AE, EM, MN, etc. along AC which are perspectively equal.

Give a drawing of the floor from another position.

Example II.   A Window

Fig. 41 shows an open leaded window, with octagonal panes.

Give a drawing of it with a change of eye-line, using the picture plane indicated in the figure (see p. 52).

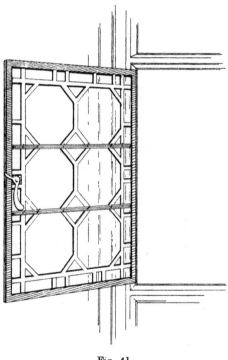

Fig. 41

REFLECTIONS OF THE SQUARE AND OCTAGON IN PLANE SURFACES

In figs. R 1 and R 2 the reflection of a square *PQRS* and its inscribed octagon *ABCDEFGH* is seen in a plane surface, which is at right angles to the P.P. and to which the side *PQ* is parallel.

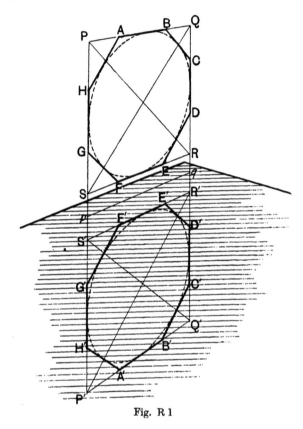

Fig. R 1

In fig. R 1 the plane of the square is at right angles to the reflecting surface and in fig. R 2 it is inclined obliquely to the reflecting surface with the side *SR* lying in it.

pq is the orthogonal projection of *PQ* on the plane. *P'* and *Q'* are the images of *P* and *Q* respectively, the straight lines *PpP'* and *QqQ'* being at right angles to the plane and therefore parallel to the P.P.

Also Pp is equal to pP', Qq is equal to qQ' and the straight line joining any other point and its image is bisected at the point in which it meets the plane. In fig. R1 these points are all in pq but in fig. R2 they lie in the sides of the rectangle $pqRS$.

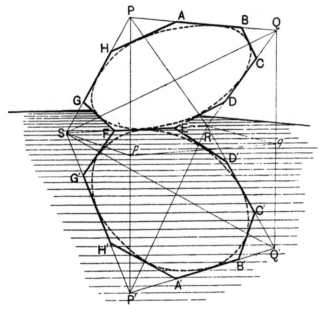

Fig. R 2

Notice that the orthogonal projections of PS and QR upon the plane, viz. pS and qR, are *horizontal and parallel* and therefore vanish at some point in the eye-line.

In both figures since PQ is parallel to the reflecting surface the image $P'Q'$ is parallel to PQ and therefore vanishes with it at some point in the eye-line.

What other straight lines in the figures vanish at this point?

THE CUBE AND SQUARE PRISM

A cube usually presents to an observer three of its faces, unequal in area and differing in light and shade. In spite of this inequality, the cube gives an impression of balance of design and of repose and stability. If some of its faces are extended so as to convert it into a square prism, many of the qualities of the figure disappear, and for this reason the cube requires for its graphical representation more care than is needed in the case of other geometrical figures.

In the preceding chapter were discussed various representations of rectangular prisms on vertical and oblique picture planes. A cube is a special case of a rectangular prism and in making a perspective drawing of a cube one is really drawing three squares in three planes at right angles to one another. These squares have a common corner and each pair has a common edge. Of the three planes in which they lie one is usually horizontal.

The case in which all the faces of the cube are inclined to a vertical picture plane may be of interest.

In fig. 42 V', V'' and V''' are the incidental vanishing points of the three sets of edges of a cube $ABCDEFGH$, the corner A being nearest to the eye of the observer. If O be the position of the eye, OV' is parallel to AD, OV'' to AB and OV''' to AE (see fig. 15).

Hence OV', OV'' and OV''' are mutually at right angles and O is the point of intersection in front of the picture plane of the three spheres which have $V'V''$, $V''V'''$ and $V'''V'$ for diameters. If the c.v.r. meets the picture plane in P it can be shown that P is the orthocentre of the triangle $V'V''V'''$.

Let us suppose the edges of the cube to be produced both ways. We shall then have three square prisms each having four faces in common with the cube.

The plane $OV'V''$ is parallel to the plane $ABCD$ and therefore at right angles to AE.

Hence the plane $OV'V''$ cuts one of the prisms in a square section which is represented in perspective by the straight line

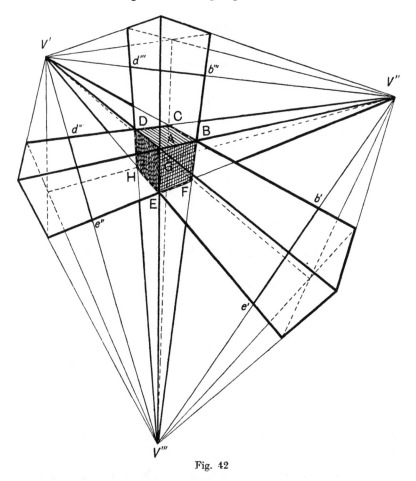

Fig. 42

$d'''b'''$. Similarly $e''d''$ and $b'e'$ are the perspective views of the sections of the other two prisms by planes through the eye.

In a view like this the direction of the eye-line is immaterial provided it passes through P, the point in which the c.v.r. meets the picture plane.

In fig. 43 the idea of intersecting square prisms is further extended. Here we have the representation of a skeleton cube. We may consider it as the drawing on an oblique picture plane (the C.V.R. being directed to the centre of the object) of a cube with one set of vertical edges, or as the drawing on a vertical picture plane of a cube with all its edges inclined to the P.P. as in fig. 42.

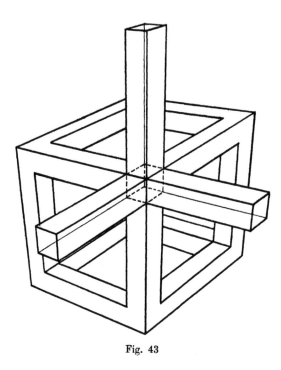

Fig. 43

Ex. The square billet moulding (p. 67) is viewed looking upwards and towards the left. Give a sketch of a small portion of it from this position.

Ex. Sketch a small portion of the nail-head moulding (p. 69) appearing as a vertical band in a jamb.

SHADOWS OF THE OCTAGONAL PRISM AND PYRAMID
IN PERSPECTIVE

In fig. 44 we have an octagonal prism resting with one octagonal face *abcdefgh* in contact with the plane A, which represents the ground plane, and surmounted by a pyramidal cap $ABCDEFGHX$, X being the vertex of the pyramid (see p. 65).

The oblique projections by the sun's rays of the points C, D, F, etc. are c', d', f', etc., so that Ccc', Ddd', Fff', etc. are typical

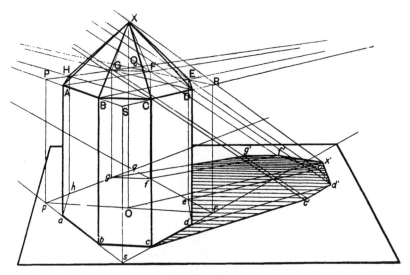

Fig. 44

equal right-angled triangles in vertical planes, whose traces on the ground plane, viz. cc', dd', ff', etc., are horizontal and parallel straight lines and therefore vanish at some point in the eye-line.

Where do Cc', Dd', etc. vanish?
Which edges of the shadow are parallel to the corresponding edges of the object?

SKETCHING

Lay tracing-paper over the following illustrations, produce the vanishing lines and thereby determine the position of the eye-line.

Example I. A Renaissance Shaft

The view taken is one looking up the shaft and for its perspective representation an oblique picture plane has been chosen. The attention is centred on *a portion* of the column and therefore the liberty is taken of using such a picture plane and not a vertical one, which would be selected for the representation of the whole.

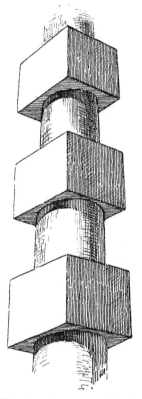

Fig. 45. Renaissance Shaft

Here the vertical lines vanish upwards at a point above the eye-line and the horizontal edges of the blocks vanish at points on the observer's horizon.

Draw from memory on an oblique picture plane the portion of the shaft as viewed from a position looking down upon it.

This doubtful ornament to a shaft is sometimes seen in Renaissance work and is quite common in modern buildings.

Example II.   A Moulding

This moulding is considered to be composed of blocks, each with one square face.   These faces lie in three planes, one of which is vertical and the other two oblique, the planes forming three sides of a regular octagonal prism whose axis is horizontal.

One set of horizontal and parallel straight lines vanishes at a point on the horizon.

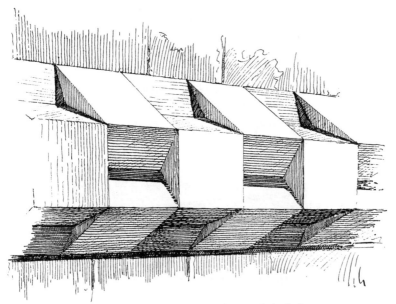

Fig. 46.   Moulding in Winchester Cathedral

The vertical sides of the central squares are therefore represented by straight lines at right angles to the eye-line, whilst the parallel oblique sides of the other squares vanish at incidental points not in the eye-line.

Test the vanishing of the parallel diagonals of the square faces.

After you have carefully considered the above statements draw the figure from memory, but in your drawing show a change in the direction of the sunlight.

An example of this moulding is found in Winchester Cathedral. It is an interesting instance of Norman work.

Example III.   A Portcullis

The structure of which this portcullis is a part is being viewed with a vertical picture plane and thus the portcullis itself is also drawn with a vertical picture plane.

Fig. 47

The vertical and horizontal edges of the bars of the wooden frame form squares which lie in vertical planes.   As the picture plane is vertical these vertical lines are drawn at right angles to the eye-line and all the horizontal lines vanish at a point on the horizon.

Draw the portcullis as seen when standing a short distance in front of the threshold with the picture plane oblique and the c.v.r. centrally situated (see fig. 68).

A portcullis is a framework made of strong bars, and movable upwards or downwards in vertical grooves inside the entrance to a fortified building. It was so adjusted as to be readily lowered when the occupants of the building had to guard against a sudden attack. The ancients had a form of portcullis in stone. In the pyramid of Dahsur there is seen the cavity for a portcullis. It rose obliquely at the side, so that the massive sealing stone slid down the incline and closed the passage. The representation of a portcullis is a favourite badge of the Tudors.

Example IV.　A Pyramid

The subsidiary figure (50) shows the directions of horizontal lines on the faces of the pyramid. These lines may represent those of the masonry, which are often plainly visible.

Two sets of horizontal lines are shown vanishing at points in the eye-line and it is most important to observe the variation in the angle contained by two of these lines which lie in the same horizontal plane.

Draw the figure from memory, arranging your shading lines to agree with the directions indicated.

Fig. 48

Figs. 49 (a) and (b) are given to show that if the base be rectangular and not square, and the walls have equal slope, the latter do not meet at a point. The mastaba shown stands on a rectangular base, and the two longer sloping sides meet in a straight line. The stepped pyramid is square in base, and the sloping sides of each stage meet at a point in the common axis.

W. & R.　　　　　　　　　　　　　　　　　13

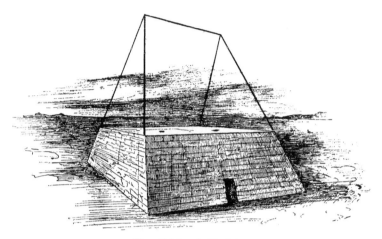

Fig. 49 (a). A Mastaba

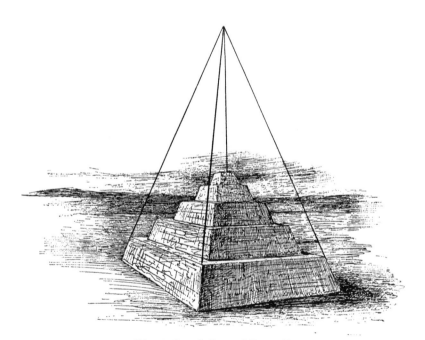

Fig. 49 (b). A Stepped Pyramid

The mastabas were private tombs, and are of early origin. In most cases they show negligence in their construction, being confused heaps of ill-assorted materials with coverings of solid stone. The stepped pyramid was also of very early origin. Its sides were divided horizontally into large steps with inclined faces. The height of these steps decreases progressively from the base to the summit. This building rather tends to the pyramidal form than achieves it; it is a rough sketch for a pyramid. It is probable that in the remote century of its structure men may not have learnt to fill up the angles left in their masonry, and they left their work in a condition which seems imperfect to us (see p. 1).

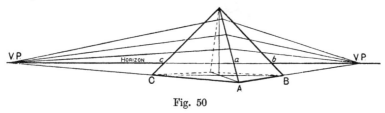

Fig. 50

Example V. Merlons

The form of one of these merlons is that of a block of square cross-section, surmounted by a larger slab which is capped by a pyramid.

In fig. 51 the picture plane is vertical and all vertical lines are consequently drawn at right angles to the eye-line.

The altitudes of the pyramids are vertical and pass through the point of intersection of the diagonals of the base.

There are two sets of *horizontal and parallel* straight lines which vanish at points in the eye-line.

Draw the figure from memory and arrange the shading lines on the faces of the pyramid to vanish.

A merlon is the solid part of a battlement and the space between the merlons is the embrasure. In the Middle Ages battlements really fulfilled their original purpose of defence and the merlons afforded protection to the defenders; later, however, battlements were placed on ecclesiastical and civil buildings for ornament.

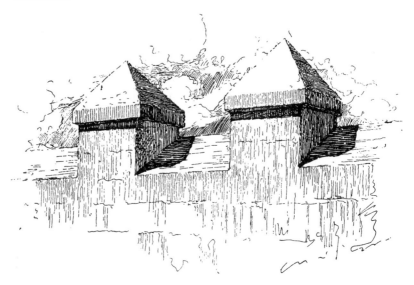

Fig. 51. Merlons with Pyramidal Caps

Example VI. A Tower

The base of the tower is square in section; the upper portion is octagonal and is surmounted by a pyramidal cap. In making a drawing of it at least one of the octagons suggested in the sketch should be constructed in full detail. Remember that in each octagon there are four pairs of *horizontal and parallel* sides vanishing at points on the horizon. The picture plane is vertical and therefore all vertical lines are drawn at right angles to the eye-line, the altitude of the pyramid being coincident with the axis of the tower.

Reproduce the sketch from memory, taking care to make the lines of the shading on the faces of the pyramid vanish at points in the eye-line.

The drawing shown is that of the church tower at Cogges in Oxfordshire.

Fig. 52.   Church Tower at Cogges, Oxfordshire, *c.* 1350

CHAPTER VII

THE TRIANGLE AND HEXAGON

Let us consider some simple geometrical properties of the equilateral triangle and its inscribed hexagon with the view to their treatment in perspective.

In fig. 53 abc is the triangle and $ABCDEF$ is the enclosed hexagon, in which

$$\hat{a} = \hat{\beta},$$
$$c\hat{X}a = 90°,$$

EA, cX, DB are parallel,

$aA = AB = Bb$; $AX = XB$,

DA bisects XY in the point O,

ED, FC and ab are parallel.

The opposite sides of the hexagon are parallel.

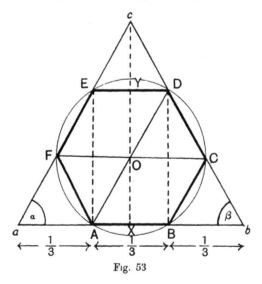

Fig. 53

In fig. 54 the hexagon lies in a horizontal plane with one pair of sides parallel to the picture plane.

Draw ab parallel to the eye-line (Law II, Cor.). Trisect ab in A and B and bisect AB in X.

Since cXa is a right angle, Xc, AE and BD vanish at the c.v. (Law I).

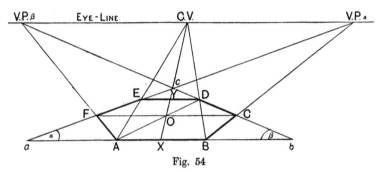

Fig. 54

Join DA cutting Xc in O and through O draw FC parallel to the eye-line. Complete the figure.

The position of c along Xc completely controls the shape of the triangle when ab is fixed. As this is the case a careful judgment of the position of c must be made.

Where do AF and CD vanish and also FE and BC?

Since ac and bc are equally inclined to the picture plane their vanishing points in the eye-line are equidistant from the c.v.

For confirmatory purposes this fact may be of use.

In fig. 55 the hexagon lies in a horizontal plane with none of its sides parallel to the picture plane.

Draw ab vanishing at v.p. 1, and divide it by the method of fig. 6, Part II, so that $aA = AB = Bb$ and $AX = XB$.

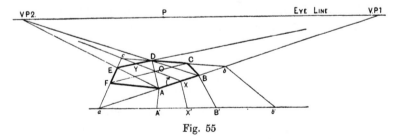

Fig. 55

Carefully judge the right angle cXA in perspective and also the position of c along Xc since they materially control the shape of the figure. Let Xc, AE and BD vanish at v.p. 2. Join DA cutting cX in O, and through O draw FC to vanish at v.p. 1. Complete the hexagon. Test the vanishing of FE, AD and BC; and also of AF and CD.

In the case of the horizontal joints of a hexagonal shaft, the figure closes as it approaches the eye-line and $c\hat{X}a$ diminishes to zero.

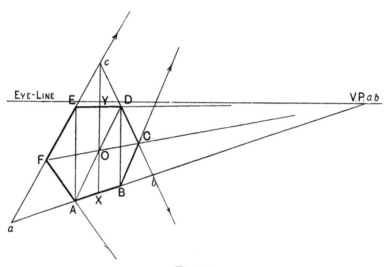

Fig. 56

In fig. 56 the hexagon is in a vertical plane with one pair of parallel sides horizontal.

Draw ab to vanish at v.p. ab, and divide it as before by the stated method.

From X draw Xc at right angles to the eye-line. AE and BD are also at right angles to the eye-line. Join AD cutting Xc in O and through O draw FC to vanish at v.p. ab. Complete the hexagon.

Where do FE and BC vanish, and also DC and FA?
What other lines vanish with them at these points?
How are the positions of these points related to v.p. ab?

Compare the vanishings of these parallel oblique lines with those of the edges of the roofs in fig. 12 (b), Part II.

Invert the figure and examine these vanishings when the hexagon is entirely above the eye-line.

SHADOWS OF THE HEXAGON IN PERSPECTIVE

In fig. 57 the hexagon $ABCDEF$ is lying in a plane parallel to the H.P. and $abcdef$ is its orthogonal projection on the H.P. (see p. 76). The projectors Aa, Bb, etc. are vertical and are therefore drawn at right angles to the eye-line. Aa', Bb', etc. represent the sun's rays and vanish at the sun, $a'b'c'd'e'f'$ being the shadow on the H.P. Typical parallel vertical planes are Aaa', Bbb', etc., and their horizontal traces aa', bb', etc. on the H.P. are therefore parallel and vanish at a point in the eye-line.

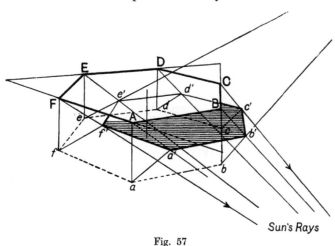

Fig. 57

We have here three sets of six *horizontal and parallel* straight lines, whose vanishing should be tested. One set is AB, ab, $a'b'$, ED, ed, $e'd'$.

What are the other two sets?

What is the position of the sun with respect to the spectator, if it is represented as in the figure by a point below the eye-line?

Ex. With the construction shown for fig. 55 make a similar drawing, showing the shadow of a hexagon in a horizontal plane with the sun behind the P.P. and with one pair of its sides parallel to the P.P. It is important that the edges of the shadow should vanish with the corresponding edges of the figure.

In fig. 58 the plane of the hexagon *ABCDEF* is vertical and *a'b'c'd'e'f'* is its shadow on the H.P. (see p. 75). One pair of sides of the hexagon, viz. *ED* and *AB*, are horizontal and the sun is behind the P.P. *a*, *b*, etc. are the orthogonal projections of *A*, *B*, etc. on the H.P., so are drawn at right angles to the eye-line. The horizontal traces on the H.P. of the parallel vertical shadow planes

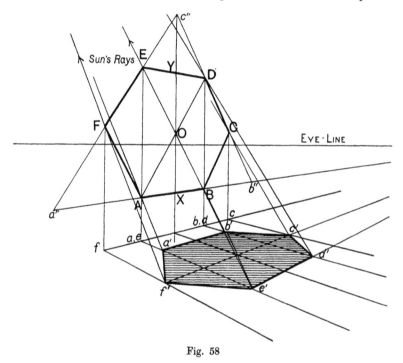

Fig. 58

Aaa', *Bbb'*, etc. are parallel and vanish at a point in the eye-line. The sun's rays vanish at a point above the eye-line.

What straight lines in the figure vanish with *AB*?

Ex. Draw the shadow when the hexagon is in a similar position, but illuminated by the sun on the near side. Use the method of construction given for fig. 56.

Ex. Fig. 100 (Part I) appears on the front of an altar cloth. Give a sketch of it as viewed from the right.

Ex. The 'lotus' band (p. 79) is seen as a horizontal border above the eye-line. Sketch it, using the construction of fig. 5. Enclose your hexagon by an ellipse for confirming your work.

TRIANGULAR AND HEXAGONAL FORMS IN PERSPECTIVE

In the two following examples make bold sketches. Use tracing-paper to find the vanishing points and eye-line of fig. 59.

Example I. A Floor

Fig. 59 shows part of a floor laid with hexagonal tiles. Use tracing-paper to determine the eye-line and the vanishing points of the three sets of horizontal and parallel sides of the hexagons.

Give a drawing of a corner of a room of which the walls only are faced with hexagonal tiles. See fig. 56.

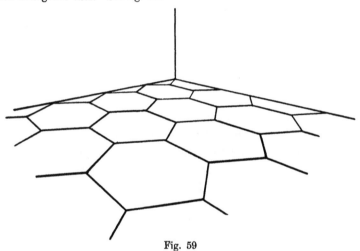

Fig. 59

Example II. Gables

Three gable fronts are shown of equal span and pitch (fig. 60). The base line AD has been divided by the method of fig. 6, Chap. v, into six equal parts, and at P, Q and R equal vertical altitudes Pp', Qq' and Rr' have been drawn. Use tracing-paper to show the directions of vanishing of the two sets of oblique parallel straight lines. If AD has been divided accurately and $p'q'r'$ vanishes with AD at a point v.p. 1 in the eye-line, then the oblique sides will vanish accurately at two incidental vanishing points.

Give a drawing of the three fronts when the eye sees slightly less of them and is situated a little above $p'q'r'$.

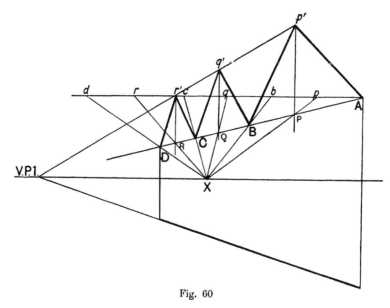

Fig. 60

REFLECTIONS OF HEXAGONS AT PLANE SURFACES AS VIEWED
WITH THE C.V.R. HORIZONTAL

In figs. R1 and R2 the reflection of a hexagon $ABCDEF$ is
seen in a plane surface which is at right angles to the P.P. The
side AB lies in the surface. In fig. R1 the plane of the hexagon is
at right angles to and in fig. R2 inclined obliquely to the reflecting
surface. In both figures X is the perspective middle point of AB,
abc is the equilateral triangle enclosing the hexagon, and the images
of the points C, D, etc. are shown by the points C', D', etc.

In fig. R1 the straight lines CC', DD', etc. are vertical and
are therefore drawn at right angles to the eye-line. Also all such
lines as CC', DD', etc. are bisected by ab, and therefore when
the hexagon has been drawn the points C', D', etc. are easily
obtained. The important construction line is cXc', in which
Xc' is equal to cX. This gives us the triangle abc', and then
straight lines drawn through C, D, etc. at right angles to the
eye-line determine the points C', D', etc.

In fig. R2 the important construction line is Xc'', which
with ab defines the H.P. $cc''c'$ is then drawn at right angles to the
eye-line, and $c'c''$ made equal to cc''. The triangle abc' can now
be drawn and the points C', D', etc. determined as in fig. R1.

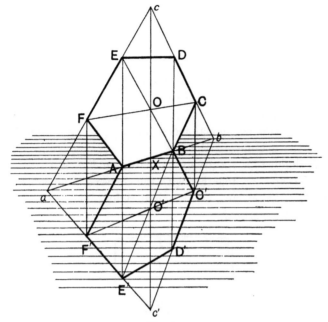

Fig. R 1

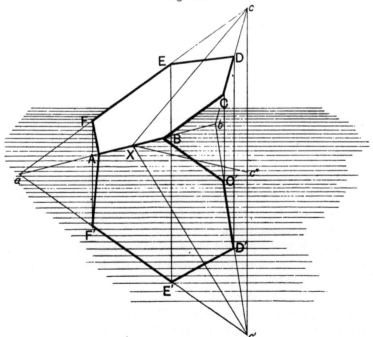

Fig. R 2

TRIANGULAR AND HEXAGONAL PRISMS AND PYRAMIDS

Two hexagonal prisms are shown in perspective, the lower one with its enclosing triangular prism.

The *horizontal and parallel* sides ab and $a'b'$ vanish at a point in the eye-line to the right of the spectator with other horizontal lines of the two hexagonal faces, and aa', bb', etc. vanish at a point in the eye-line to the left.

ab is divided perspectively as shown in fig. 56.

AE, BD and Xc, together with the corresponding construction lines on the further face, are drawn at right angles to the eye-line, since they are vertical.

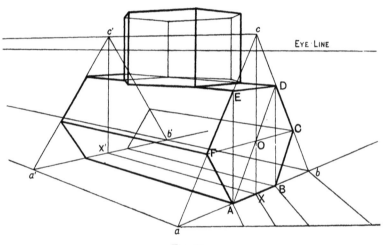

Fig. 61

AD is joined to cut cX in O, and FOC is drawn to vanish with ab. The vertices of the hexagon are thus determined.

Ex. Examine with tracing-paper the vanishing of the oblique edges, and reproduce the whole figure showing the construction in full of the upper prism.

Observe how the parallel planes of the hexagonal ends vanish, the near face appearing more closed than the one more removed from the spectator.

Ellipses may be sketched to enclose the two hexagons, thus giving a cylinder in perspective. This shows more clearly the variation in the apparent openness of the figures.

PERSPECTIVE VIEWS OF A TRIANGULAR PRISM

We have shown here a series of perspective representations of a triangular prism (fig. 62). The triangular faces of the prism lie in vertical planes and are isosceles, with their bases horizontal. Five positions are considered and their perspective representations are numbered i, ii, iii, iv and v.

OX bisects at right angles the base of one of the triangular faces, and the prism is rotated about OX. The c.v.r. is directed to a point in OX produced.

In position i OA is parallel to the picture plane and therefore $X\hat{O}A$ is a right angle.

Where do the edges which are at right angles to the triangular faces vanish?

As the prism is rotated about OX, the length of OA decreases from position i to position iii, where it has its least value. The apparent lengths of OA are controlled by the apparent lengths of the radii of a horizontal circle of which O is the centre.

After position iv the other triangular face becomes visible.

Notice that the right angle XOA in position i increases to two right angles in position iii, and note carefully the changes in the three right angles shown at the point O.

In fig. 63 the prism is supposed to be rotated about the base of one of its triangular faces. This base is kept horizontal and is shown by OX, O being its middle point. OY lies in the adjacent rectangular face and is at right angles to OX.

Five positions are shown. In positions i and v OY is vertical, so that OA and OE are horizontal, whilst in position iv the altitude of the shaded triangle has its least value. Here the apparent lengths of this altitude are controlled by the apparent lengths of the radii of a vertical circle whose plane is at right angles to OX.

During the rotation of the prism the edge PQ remains parallel to OX and therefore always vanishes with it at the same point in the eye-line.

In positions ii, iii and iv the short edges of the prism vanish at incidental points.

What is the locus of these incidental points?

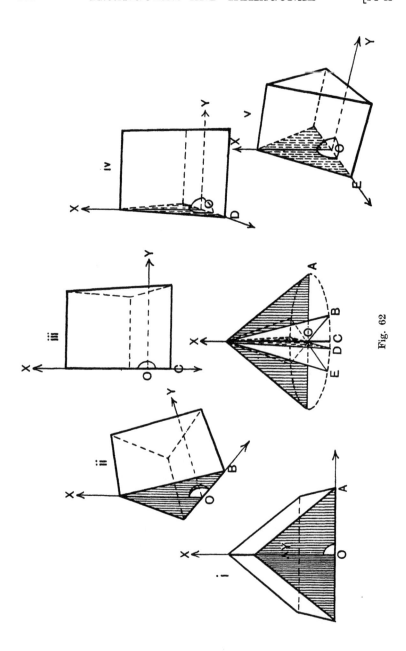

Fig. 62

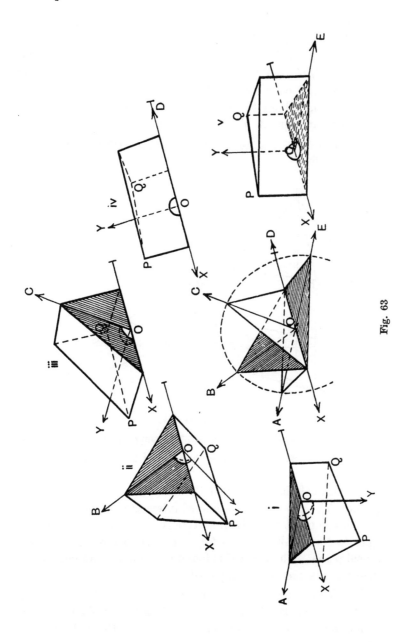

Fig. 63

In fig. 64 we have in perspective a regular triangular prism *ABCDEF* standing with its triangular face *ABC* in contact with the ground (see p. 85). On the upper face *DEF* rests a triangular pyramid *DEFG*, and the whole casts a shadow in sunlight on the ground and on a vertical plane.

The sun is behind the spectator, so the sun's rays *Gg'*, *Dd'*, etc. vanish at a point below the eye-line.

If *G'g'* is the horizontal trace of the vertical plane *GG'g'*, where does *G'g'* meet the eye-line?

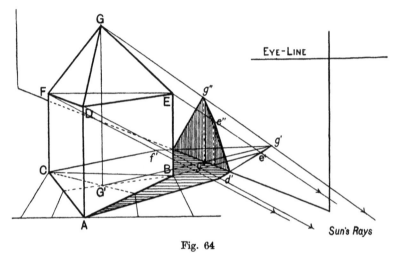

Fig. 64

Horizontal traces of other typical vertical planes are *Ad'*, *Be'*, *Cf'* and *d'*, *e'*, *f'*, *g'* are the shadows of the points *D, E, F, G* on the ground.

The vertical plane on which the shadow is also received cuts *f'g'* and *d'e'*. *G'g'* meets its line of intersection with the ground plane in the point *g'''*. Then a vertical line *g'''g''*, drawn at right angles to the eye-line, meets *Gg'* in *g''*, the shadow of *G* on this vertical plane. The point *e''* is found in a similar manner, and the shadow edges are then completed.

Ex. Make a drawing of a triangular prism and its pyramidal cap standing on the ground plane and casting a shadow on the ground and a vertical wall when the sun is to the right in front of the spectator.

Fig. 65 shows in perspective a regular hexagonal prism (with its enclosing triangular prism) lying with one rectangular face on the ground plane.   The face $ABCDEF$ is the base of a regular hexagonal pyramid $GABCDEF$.   The sun is in front of the spectator, and therefore the sun's rays Cc', Dd', etc. vanish at a point above the eye-line.

Ae', Bd', etc. are the horizontal and parallel traces of the parallel vertical planes AEe', BDd', etc., which contain the sun's rays, and vanish at a point in the eye-line.

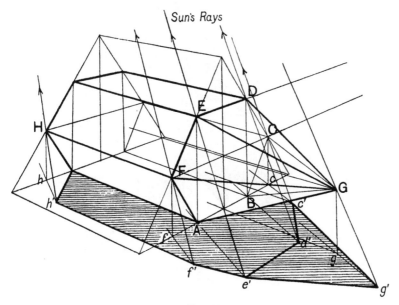

Fig. 65

How is this point connected with the vanishing point of Ee', Dd', etc.?

Show how, if the directions of the sun's rays are already drawn, the horizontal traces Ae', Bd', etc. may be constructed.

Ex. A dove-cot of the form of the figure on p. 91 is viewed well above the eye-line. Sketch it, adding interesting surroundings.

SKETCHING

The following examples are intended to illustrate the principles of construction explained in this chapter.

14—2

Example I.   A Headstone

The form of the stone suggests a combination of triangular and rectangular prisms.

There are two sets of *horizontal and parallel* straight lines, which vanish on the eye-line on either side of the spectator, and since the picture plane is vertical, the vertical edges of the stone

Fig. 66

are at right angles to the eye-line.   The oblique edges vanish at incidental points above and below the eye-line.

(i)   Use tracing-paper to show that these two points are on a line which is at right angles to the eye-line and passes through the vanishing point of the base lines of the triangular faces.

(ii)   Draw in light and shade, using an oblique picture plane, a three-quarter view looking downwards, the sun casting a shadow towards you.

This simple headstone is probably fifteenth century work, and is found in Handborough Churchyard in Oxfordshire.

Example II.   A Roman Coffin

In this example we have a form similar to that in Example I. The view taken is that seen by the spectator looking downwards, with the picture plane oblique, since it is being considered as a whole and not as one of a group of objects. A photograph of the object taken with the lens directed down towards its centre would show a similar arrangement of lines, if the plate were in a plane at right angles to the axis of the lens.

Fig. 67.   Roman Coffin, York

The vertical sides vanish at a point below the eye-line in the straight line which passes through the central point of the object and is at right angles to the eye-line (Law IV); whilst there are two sets of *horizontal and parallel* straight lines which vanish at points on the eye-line on either side of the spectator.

Draw in light and shade, with a vertical picture plane, a three-quarter view of the coffin with the longer edges vanishing to the left. Insert some artistic effect to suggest antiquity.

This example is of the Roman period and was found at York. To this kind of tomb, or rather stone coffin, the name ' sarcophagus ' is usually applied. In some cases, as at Westminster, it has been used again at later times.

Example III. An Opening

This opening has been drawn from a view directed upwards with an oblique picture plane, whose line of intersection with the plane of the wall is horizontal.

Fig. 68. Opening, Deerhurst Church, Gloucestershire

In the figure the vertical lines vanish at a point above the eye-line, since the plane of the wall recedes upwards. The horizontal lines of the wall are all parallel to the picture plane and are drawn parallel to the eye-line; and there is also one set of horizontal lines which vanishes at a point in the eye-line. (See figs. 1 (*b*) and 15, Part II.)

Give a drawing in light and shade of the opening, with an oblique picture plane, looking down from above.

This example is of supposed Saxon origin.

Example IV. A Church

This view is taken from a height and drawn with an oblique picture plane.

The vertical planes recede downwards and all vertical lines vanish at a point on a line passing through the c.v. at right angles to the eye-line. (See fig. 23 (*b*).)

Fig. 69

There are, as usual, two sets of *horizontal and parallel* straight lines which vanish at points in the eye-line.

With an oblique picture plane draw a view of the church when facing the east end and looking downwards along the central line of the nave. Show shadows when the sun is in the west.

Example V. A Wall

Coping stones and bricks are shown in the figure. There are two sets of horizontal and parallel straight lines vanishing at the eye-line on either side of the spectator, and some oblique parallels vanishing at incidental points.

Give a sketch from the other side of the wall showing the upper portion of the buttress.

Fig. 70

Example VI.   A Conduit-house

The figure shows a stone hexagonal conduit-house at Abingdon in Berkshire, with a small gable over the doorway.

One pair of the vertical sides is parallel to the picture plane (see fig. 54) and there are construction lines which vanish at the c.v.

How would you find on tracing-paper the exact position of the c.v. ?

Fig. 70 (a)

Make a clear line ruled drawing of all the main lines of the building, showing eye-line, vanishing points and construction lines. After you have done this, give a memory sketch of the house and foliage as seen from any other position.

CHAPTER VIII

THE CIRCLE

According to the direction in which a circle is viewed it appears as a circle, straight line, or ellipse. When the c.v.r. passes through the centre of the circle and is at right angles to its plane, the circle presents its true circular form. It appears as a straight line when the eye lies in the plane of the circle. In any other position its apparent form is elliptical.

In figs. 127 and 128 (Part I), a geometrical projection of the circle has been given, and it is proposed to discuss a similar method for perspective projection.

There cannot be much doubt about the difficulty of drawing a circle in perspective with even fair accuracy. There are two main reasons for this.

Most beginners have never observed the existence of a 'tilt,' —the inclination of the greater axis of the ellipse to the eye-line or to a line at right angles to the eye-line—or the variation of this tilt as the eye changes its position. One difficulty lies here,— the correct rendering of the tilt. The other is the delineation of the curve of the ellipse, the forming of a curve truly symmetrical about its greater and smaller axes.

We can learn a great deal by enclosing the circle in a suitably placed square and using an 'eight-point' method for the construction of the ellipse. The tilt will be shown correctly, provided the square has been correctly drawn. At the outset this mechanical means will be of great help to the beginner in seeing for himself how the tilt varies. After some practice he may dispense with it.

Common faults in the delineation of the ellipse are the exaggeration of the curvature at the ends of the greater axis and the underrating of the curvature at the ends of the smaller axis.

In fig. 71 we have shown in perspective a square enclosing a circle lying in a horizontal plane.

The sides of the square $EFGH$ vanish at points V' and V'' in the eye-line, and the diagonals intersect in O. The straight lines AOC and DOB vanish with the sides of the square. A is joined to X, the perspective middle point of BE, and EC is drawn; the intersection of these two straight lines gives a required point P on the circle. To confirm the position of X observe that AX and HB are parallel and therefore vanish at some point in the eye-line.

PV' is drawn to vanish at V', cutting AF in Q.

QV'' is drawn to vanish at V'', cutting AG in R.

RV' is drawn to vanish at V', cutting HC in S.

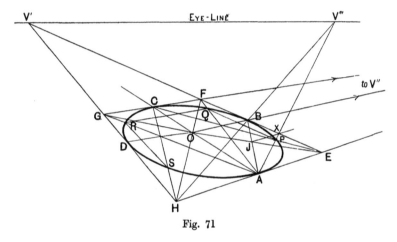

Fig. 71

The ellipse is now drawn through the eight points A, B, C, D, P, Q, R and S to touch the sides of the square at A, B, C and D.

Make a tracing of the ellipse and the eye-line of fig. 71. On the tracing-paper draw two tangents to the ellipse parallel to the eye-line, and draw the straight line through their points of contact to meet the eye-line in the c.v. This straight line should pass through the point O, and it can be proved that it contains the geometrical centre of the ellipse. From the c.v. draw the two tangents to the ellipse. The sides of an enclosing square are thus obtained.

By the method just described obtain the eight points. It
will be easier to arrange the point X in the side of the square
nearest to the eye, since this side is parallel to the P.P. You will
find that these eight points lie on the ellipse and that the diagonals
of the square pass through the point O.

We thus see that the same ellipse is obtained regardless of
the enclosing square that we select and this selected square should
be so placed as to provide the greatest economy of lines. Further,
in drawing this square, the 'openness' of the ellipse which is controlled by the ratio of its axes is to be taken into account. The
more open the square, the more open will be the ellipse, and the
longer the sides of the square, the longer will be the greater axis
of the ellipse.

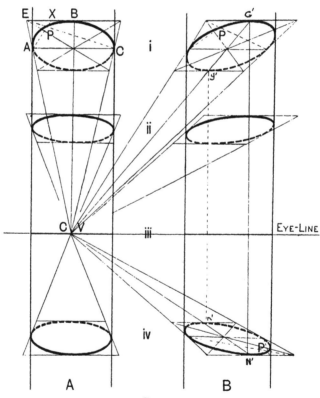

Fig. 72

Fig. 72 shows two cylindrical shafts (A and B) in perspective.

The c.v. of the observer is shown on the axial line of A, on which four horizontal circles are drawn. Four are also drawn on B. The selected enclosing squares have sides parallel to the p.p. and the points corresponding to X of fig. 71 are taken in the near sides which are parallel to the eye-line. The point P is the intersection of EC and AX. The ellipses of A show no tilt, but those of B do, and we notice that in this case the tilt varies with the distance of the ellipse from the eye-line. It will also vary with the distance of the shaft to the right or left of the spectator, except in the case of iii.

If we now direct our vision to the axial line of B and thus change our picture plane, the ellipses in B show no tilt.

How may a circle move showing no variation in tilt?

Regarding the openness of the ellipses we observe that it decreases as they approach the eye-line, where it vanishes.

Here we have been considering circles in horizontal planes only, and we leave the correct drawing of the circle in oblique planes to the student.

We shall find the drawing of circles in vertical planes somewhat simpler.

Turn fig. 72 round so that the axial line of A becomes a new eye-line. We now have circles in parallel vertical planes, and notice that the ellipses with their centres on the eye-line have no tilt, whilst in other cases the tilt varies with the distance above or below the eye-line except in case iii, and with the distance to the right or left of the spectator.

Ex. Show in perspective an upper corner of a room having a wide decorated frieze, the basis of the design for which consists of a row of equal tangential circles.

Circular Forms

Example I. A Floor

Fig. 73 represents the scheme of a design for an ornamental floor.

Make a tracing of the figure and on it rule the greater axes of the five ellipses, showing the tilt of each.

What do you observe concerning the change of tilt?

The point P has been obtained by the method already described.

Make a drawing of this arrangement of circles in a horizontal plane when the sides of the squares vanish one on either side of the spectator.

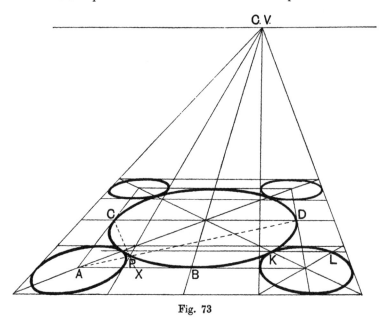

Fig. 73

Example II.   An Arcade

Fig. 74 represents a series of arches showing semicircles in a vertical plane, whose radii are equal to the height of the supports.

The method of obtaining the points P is shown. Since the centres lie near the eye-line there is but little tilt and as the circles recede the openness decreases.

On tracing-paper draw the nearest arch and support. Remove the figure and on the tracing-paper draw the next two, using the method of fig. 6, Part II. Replace the tracing-paper to confirm your work.

Example III.   A Ceiling

Fig. 75 shows a circle which may form a part of the scheme of ornamentation of a ceiling. It might also suggest the base circle of a lantern. The square selected has its sides parallel to the sides of the room, and the construction of P is shown, from which three other points can be readily obtained.

Draw the complete figure with one of the wall lines perpendicular to the picture plane.

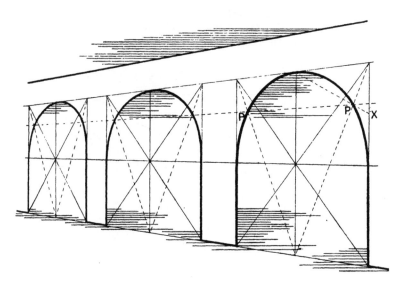

Fig. 74

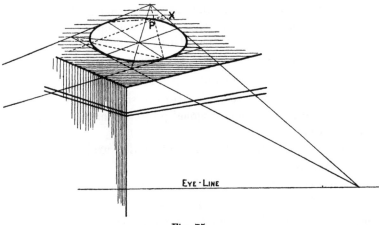

Fig. 75

Example IV. Tiles

The figure shows the arrangement of semicircular tiles on a roof, a few only of which are drawn (see fig. 134, Part ɪ).

On tracing-paper mark clearly the eye-line and the incidental vanishing points of any series of parallel oblique lines on the roof and also the construction lines for the drawing of one semicircle.

Make a drawing of a few of the tiles of the roof when the line of the eaves is parallel to the picture plane.

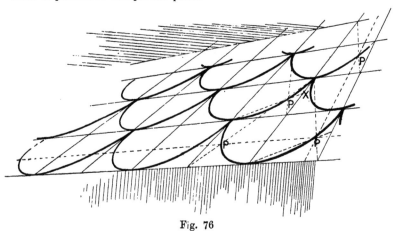

Fig. 76

SHADOWS OF CIRCLES

In fig. 77 we have the perspective representation of a circle lying in a horizontal plane and casting a shadow on the ground plane (see p. 99). We have chosen an enclosing square with one pair of sides, AD and BC, parallel to the picture plane. These are therefore drawn parallel to the eye-line.

Where do CD and BA vanish?

The directions of the sun's rays are shown by Aa', Bb', Cc' and Dd', and $abcd$ is the orthogonal projection of $ABCD$ upon the ground plane.

aa', bb', etc. being horizontal and parallel straight lines vanish at a point in the eye-line.

How is this point connected with the vanishing point of Aa', Bb', etc.?

The shadow may be conveniently obtained by projecting the enclosing square $ABCD$ on the ground plane by straight lines drawn through the vanishing point of the sun's rays, and then drawing the inscribed circle in the projected square by the method of fig. 71.

If the sun is in front of the spectator, as in the figure, the openness of the shadow is greater than that of the circle itself.

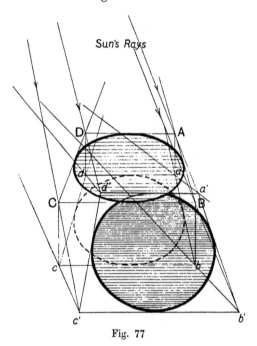

Fig. 77

Fig. 78 shows in perspective a circle in a vertical plane enclosed in a square $ABCD$ and casting a shadow on the ground and on a vertical plane B (see p. 99). AD and BC are vertical whilst AB and DC are horizontal and vanish at a point in the eye-line.

The sun's rays are represented by Aa', Bb', Cc' and Dd', and vanish at a point above the eye-line. $a'b'c'd'$ is the shadow on the ground of the square $ABCD$. $a'd'$ and $b'c'$ are *horizontal and parallel* and vanish at some point in the eye-line.

What is the figure $a'b'c'd'$ in reality?   Where do $b'a'$ and $c'd'$ vanish?

The plane B is introduced to contain AD and pass through e', the middle point of the side $a'b'$. This is the point in which the shadow touches $a'b'$. The shadow of AB on the plane B is

Ae', and hence that of the circle touches Ae' at e' and the circle at the middle point of AD.

Ex. Sketch an equilateral arch (fig. 147, Part I) as viewed above the eye-line.   Show in perspective the full construction of two intersecting semicircles.

Ex. An encircled Greek cross is carved in low relief on a grave-stone which lies in a horizontal plane.   Give a sketch of it when viewed *directly* from a position a few yards from it (see fig. 85).

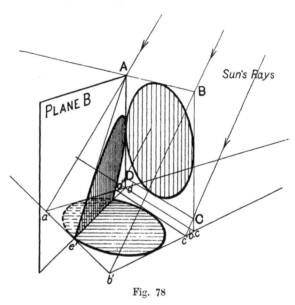

Fig. 78

REFLECTIONS OF CIRCLES IN PERSPECTIVE

In fig. R 1 three equal circles A, B and C are shown with their centres in the same vertical line.   The circles are enclosed by squares two of whose sides are vertical, the two remaining sides vanishing at a point in the eye-line. xy is a horizontal line lying in the ground plane.

The circle C has its centre on the eye-line and is enclosed by the square $abcd$. ad and bc are vertical lines and meet the ground plane in x and y respectively.   On them lengths xd' and yc' are made equal to xd or yc, also xa' and yb' equal to xa or yb.   Then $a'b'c'd'$ is the reflection of the square $abcd$, and its inscribed circle

D is the reflection of the circle C in the ground plane. The reflection E of B in the same plane is also shown.

Notice that in this figure any circle below the eye-line can be

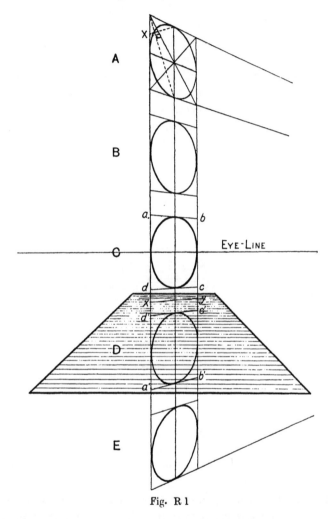

Fig. R 1

made to represent the reflection of any other of the circles, by choosing xy, the straight line in the ground plane, to bisect the distance between the centres of the circles.

Observe the difference of tilt of the object and its image.

Fig. R 2 shows the reflection of a circle in an oblique plane, the circumference touching the plane.

The sides *ab* and *dc* of the enclosing square are horizontal. *axa'* and *byb'* are vertical straight lines through *a* and *b*, and *ax*, *xa'*, *by* and *yb'* are of equal length.

Thus *a'b'cd* is the reflection in the ground plane of the square *abcd*, and the inscribed circle is the reflection of the circle inscribed in *abcd*. Since any point of the circle gives a reflected point which is as much below the ground plane as the point is above it, we can easily obtain the reflection of several points on the circle (e.g. those lying on the diagonals of the square), instead of directly constructing the circle in the square *a'b'cd*.

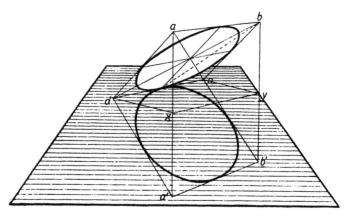

Fig. R 2

Ex. An old stone bridge with one semicircular arch spans a narrow stream. Give an artistic sketch of it when viewed from the bank near the bridge, and with the planes of the semicircles vanishing to the left. Show the reflection of the arch in the stream (see p. 227).

Ex. A circular fish-pond with a stone edge is viewed *directly* from a position a few yards from it. Give a sketch of it showing that part of the reflection of the edge seen in the water (see fig. 85).

THE SPHERE, CONE, CYLINDER AND RING

Let us now consider the perspective representation of some solids of circular section. In most cases this depends on the correct drawing in perspective of some circle or circles whose position is well known. In dealing with the sphere, however, a difficulty arises. The rays of light from the sphere to the eye of the spectator are bounded by a right circular cone, the axis of which is, in general, oblique to the picture plane. The projection of the sphere on the picture plane is therefore an ellipse, and the difficulty lies in fixing the position and limits of the circular section of the sphere which is touched by the cone of visual rays. To avoid this difficulty it is usual to represent a sphere in perspective by a circle.

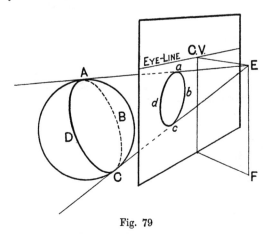

Fig. 79

In the figure *EF* represents the spectator and *abcd* the perspective representation on a vertical picture plane of the sphere shown. The tangent lines from *E* to the sphere meet its surface at points on the circumference of the circle *ABCD* and trace out a right circular cone with *E* for vertex. *abcd* is the section of this cone by the picture plane. It will be seen that the perspective projection of the sphere is the same as that of the circle *ABCD*, the plane of which is at right angles to the straight line joining its centre to the point *E*. Hence the figure *abcd* is an ellipse except when the centre of the sphere lies on the c.v.r.

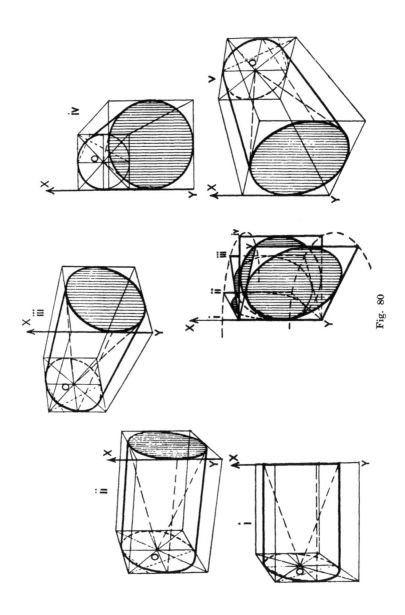

Fig. 80

Refer to fig. 72. Two tall cylinders are shown in perspective, projected on a common vertical plane. They are observed as a group, with the c.v. on one of the axes, and are drawn as a photograph shows them.

In modern life, photography begins to influence the conception of forms in such a way that they are thought of as they are photographically represented; and if now a group of objects be shown, each with a separate picture plane, there arises a sense of untruthfulness in this method of representation.

In the construction of the ellipses the selected enclosing squares have in each case a pair of sides parallel to the picture plane, and half the near side of the lower square has been bisected to obtain P.

Place tracing-paper on the diagram and mark on it the greater axes in order to observe the change in tilt which has already been discussed on p. 221.

Thus for the drawing of the cylinder construct complete square prisms, and insert circles in each square face. The side lines of the cylinder are tangential to both curves and should be parallel to the axes of the prisms.

Refer to fig. 83. Here lines GN are drawn on the curved surface of a cylinder. These lines are generators, and represent the position of the side of the rectangle which generates the cylindrical surface (see p. 110). As this line travels round the cylinder its distance from the picture plane changes from maximum at $g'n'$ to a minimum at $G'N'$. This means that its apparent length changes too, and it is this change that most students fail to understand, especially in the drawing of the 'ring.' As GN travels round the cylinder and disappears from view it becomes gradually shorter. At this stage it is most important to show imagination in rendering the perspective parallelism of the curves. In perspective theory the greatest generator is $G'N'$ (fig. 72), that which is on the face of the square prism, and therefore nearest to the picture plane. The least generator is diametrically opposite the greatest, and therefore farthest from the picture plane. This method of treatment is necessary when groups are under consideration. If on the other hand our thought is concentrated on one object of the group—say the left-hand cylinder—the picture plane changes, and the longest—

in this case the nearest—generator is immediately in front of the centres of the circles, and the tilt vanishes.

PERSPECTIVE VIEWS OF A CYLINDER

In fig. 80 we have a series of views of a square prism and its enclosed cylinder (and cone). One of the sides XY of one of the square faces is fixed in a vertical position and the prism is rotated about this line as axis. YX produced meets the eye-line in the c.v. and the positions of the nearer square face and its inscribed circle are indicated in the central figure.

In position i this face is at right angles to the picture plane and is represented by a straight line. As the cylinder rotates from position i to position iv the openness of the ellipse which represents the near circular face increases to its maximum value. The tilt varies and vanishes in positions i and iv.

Observe the difference of tilt of the near and far ellipses in each position.

The cylinder is completed by drawing tangents to the two circular faces. These straight lines should be parallel to the axis of the cylinder and to one set of edges of the prism, and should therefore vanish with them at a point in the eye-line.

In practice you may find it convenient to draw these tangents vanishing with the axis immediately after the nearer ellipse is drawn, and then to insert the further ellipse touching these two tangents and the four sides of its enclosing square, observing the difference in tilt.

Fig. 81 shows the plan of a ring and the additional construction for obtaining points on the inner circle. Join OP, and after the width WQ of the annulus is fixed, draw WT parallel to PQ. This gives T, and the remaining points can be obtained.

Fig. 82 shows the change in the perspective length of the radial intercept on the face of the ring when the centre of the circles lies on the straight line through the c.v. at right angles to the eye-line. The limits of the foreshortenings occur in those intercepts which are in line with the greatest and least generators. Of these two limits the greater, $M'G'$, is that which meets the greatest generator; also the foreshortening vanishes when the

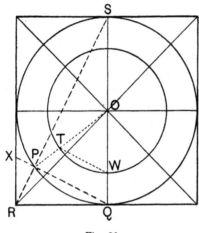

Fig. 81

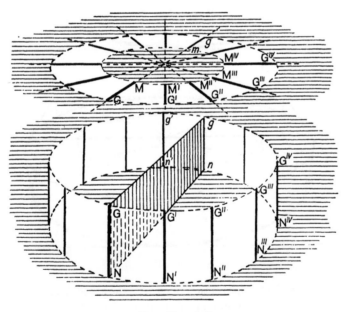

Figs. 82 and 83

intercepts are parallel to the picture plane. In this figure there is no tilt and the minor axes of the curves are coincident but the major axes are not.

In other cases, when there is tilt, neither pair of corresponding axes coincide, and the consideration of the variation in the length of the radial intercept is not simple.

To see this trace the curves of fig. 86, marking the position of the centre of the enclosing square. Draw the major and minor axes of each ellipse and the greatest and least radial intercepts.

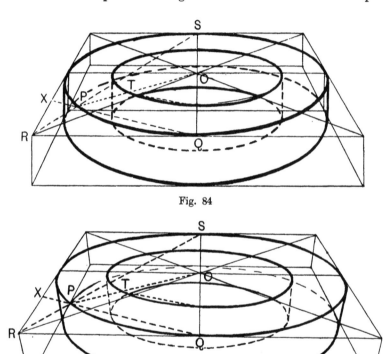

Fig. 84

Fig. 85

The method of construction is clearly shown in figs. 84 and 85, with lettering corresponding to that of fig. 81. The rings in figs. 85, 86 and 97 (a gable cross) are viewed with an oblique picture plane with the c.v.r. directed to the centre of the object, but in figs. 84 and 96 (a piscina) the objects are below a horizontal C.V.R.

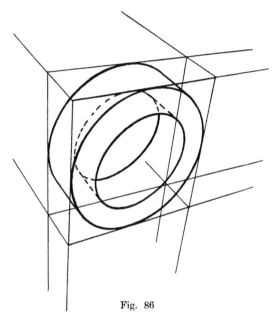

Fig. 86

SHADOWS OF THE SPHERE, CONE, CYLINDER AND RING
IN PERSPECTIVE

In fig. 87 we have shown in perspective the shadow cast on the ground by a sphere (see p. 118).

The sun's rays are represented by Aa', Bb', etc., and lie in a plane parallel to the picture plane. Hence in the drawing they are represented by parallel straight lines.

The central section of the sphere which is at right angles to the direction of the sun's rays is enclosed in a square $ABCD$, of which the sides AD and BC are parallel to the picture plane. The orthogonal projection of $ABCD$ on the plane is $abcd$ and the shadow cast by the sun is $a'b'c'd'$. Here ad and $a'd'$ are in the same straight line as also are bc and $b'c'$.

At what point do AB, $a'b'$, etc. vanish?

The shadow of the sphere is the ellipse drawn to touch the sides of $a'b'c'd'$ at their perspective middle points.

If the direction of the sun's rays is known, the direction of
AD is also known, but the fixing of the central section of the
sphere with fair accuracy is not easy and is largely a matter of
experience.

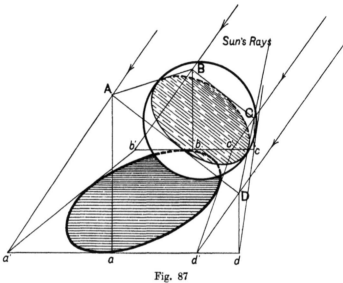

Fig. 87

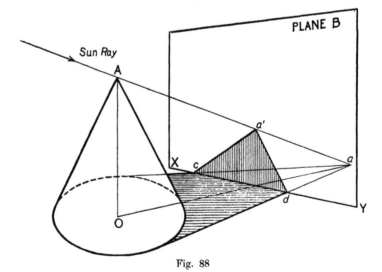

Fig. 88

The shadow of a cone on a horizontal plane and on a vertical plane B is shown in fig. 88. The cone rests with its base in contact with the horizontal plane (see p. 118). O is the centre of the base circle and A the vertex. A ray from the sun through A meets the horizontal plane in a and the plane B in a'. Tangents to the base circle from a mark the limits of the shadow on the horizontal plane; if these cut XY, the line of intersection of the two planes, in c and d then $a'c$ and $a'd$ mark the limits on the vertical plane.

Where is the c.v. in the figure?

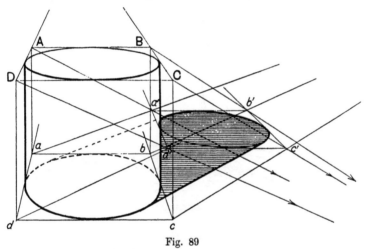

Fig. 89

In fig. 89 we have the shadow of a cylinder on a horizontal plane (see p. 119). The sun is behind the spectator and therefore the sun's rays Aa', Bb', etc. vanish at a point below the eye-line. The cylinder rests with one circular face in contact with the plane and is enclosed in a square prism four of whose edges, viz. AB, DC, ab, dc, are parallel to the picture plane.

Where do DA, CB, da, cb vanish?

The shadow of the square $ABCD$ on the plane is $a'b'c'd'$.

Where do aa', bb', etc. vanish?

The shadow of the upper circular face is the ellipse drawn to touch the sides of the figure $a'b'c'd'$ at their perspective middle points. The limits of the shadow of the cylinder are this curve and the straight lines touching both this curve and the base circle of the cylinder.

In fig. 90 we have a drawing in perspective of a short hollow cylinder or ring, which rests with its curved surface in contact with a horizontal plane. The ring is enclosed in a square prism $ABCDPQRS$, $ABCD$ being the square face nearer to the spectator. The construction lines are omitted for greater clearness. $a'b'q'p'$ is the shadow on the horizontal plane of $ABQP$, and the curves of the ellipses described in the figures $p'q'RS$ and $a'b'CD$

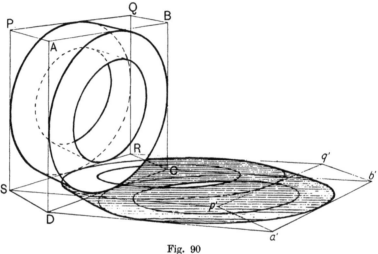

Fig. 90

and touching the sides at their perspective middle points mark the outer limits of the curved portion of the shadow. The straight edges of the shadow are obtained by drawing straight lines to touch these ellipses and to vanish with the generators of the ring.

The ellipses which are the shadows of the inner circles of the ring are described in a similar manner, and the area common to them is an area on which there is no shadow. Thus the inner limits of the shadow are obtained.

Ex. Sketch the guilloche moulding of fig. 184 (Part I) placed well above the eye-line, and with the horizontal edges of the slab vanishing at a point on the left of the c.v.

Ex. An ornamental cylindrical chimney lies a little to the right of a gable which is viewed obliquely and well above the

eye-line. The c.v. of the spectator is on the altitude of the gable.
Give a sketch with shadows of the gable and chimney (see fig. 72).

Practical Work

Fig. 91 shows a model in which is seen the method of
constructing a vault. It represents a waggon-head vault with
an intersecting vault occupying part of its length. Vaults of
the Norman period were simple barrel-headed ones, and semicircular arches only were used in their construction.

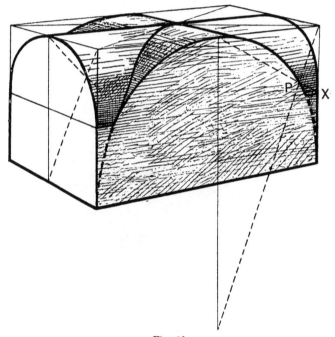

Fig. 91

Construct the model in plasticine, taking care with the intersecting lines of the half-cylinders. From the interior this line
would be conspicuous, and in more complicated vaultings this
edge was elaborately moulded, giving rise to characteristic ribs.

SKETCHING

The following examples are intended to illustrate the principles
of construction explained in this chapter.

Example I.   A Pillar

The figure represents the upper portion of a square pillar, surmounted by two square slabs and a sphere. A little difficulty will be met with in placing in true perspective the sphere at the centre of the uppermost square.

Draw the vertical diameter, the extremities of which are O, the point of contact, and T, the summit of the sphere. Slightly

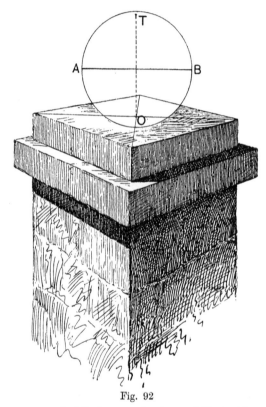

Fig. 92

below the centre of OT draw a horizontal line AB to represent the apparent breadth of the sphere, judging its length in proportion to the breadth of the slab on which it rests.

Draw the object with an oblique picture plane as seen by the eye well below the sphere, and with some edges of the pillar parallel to the picture plane. To show the visible portion of the sphere, the full construction of the top square should be made. [AB will appear above the middle point of OT.]

Example II. A Rock-cut Frieze

Three equal vertical squares are here separated by vertical bands and the far circle of each circular slab is inscribed in one of the squares.

After you have studied the features of the frieze, making mental notes of the proportion of its details, draw from memory the whole figure.

This example is taken from a rock-cut temple at Petra in North Arabia.

Fig. 93

Example III. A Roman Wall

A series of roughly hewn arches is shown, which constitute a part of the Roman wall at Cilurnum.

Fig. 94. Arches at Cilurnum

Give an artistic drawing of the wall with its main horizontal lines vanishing at a point to the left, and with the eye well below the arches. [See fig. 74, Part II.]

Example IV. The Frithstool at Beverley

This in its simplest form is a rectangular block with a semi-cylindrical hollow.

In the view shown none of the lines are perpendicular to the picture plane.

Fig. 95

You may find it necessary to enclose the complete circle by a square whose sides are parallel to the upper edges of the block.

Give a memory sketch of the figure.

Frithstools still exist at Hexham and at Beverley in the north aisle of the chancel. They provided security from punishment to fugitives from justice who claimed the privilege of sanctuary.

Example V.   A Piscina

The figure shows a piscina of conical form with enrichment.

Draw in light and shade a side view of the piscina showing the extent of its engagement with the wall (see fig. 84).

The piscina was used to receive the water in which the priest washed his hands as well as that with which the chalice was rinsed.

Fig. 96.   Piscina at Crowmarsh Church, Oxon.

In this country it is generally placed on the south side of the chancel, but in Normandy it is not unusual to find it on the north.

Examples dating from the twelfth century are rare but from the thirteenth century they are abundant.

Example **VI.** A Gable Cross

It will be convenient to consider this cross to have been cut from a square slab.

The figure has been drawn with an oblique picture plane in the manner shown in fig. 86, Part II.

Give a drawing of the cross with a vertical picture plane as seen from the same side but looking upwards.

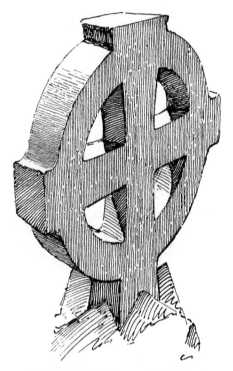

Fig. 97.   Gable Cross at Cheltenham

As an architectural feature a cross was often placed upon the tops of gables of churches. This example is taken from a church at Cheltenham, and is one of the few Norman examples that have withstood exposure for so many years (see p. 36).

INDEX TO ILLUSTRATIONS

The numbers refer to the pages

For EU product safety concerns, contact us at Calle de José Abascal, 56–1°,
28003 Madrid, Spain or eugpsr@cambridge.org.

www.ingramcontent.com/pod-product-compliance
Ingram Content Group UK Ltd.
Pitfield, Milton Keynes, MK11 3LW, UK
UKHW030855150625
459647UK00021B/2803